IVAN
MASSOW'S
GAY FINANCE
GUIDE

FOURTH ESTATE
LONDON

I owe this book to
Digby Larner and his charming wife Judith,
without whose help and support it would
never have been written

First published in Great Britain in 1994 by
Fourth Estate Limited
289 Westbourne Grove
London W11 2QA

A catalogue record for this book is available
from the British Library.

ISBN 1–85702–165–7

Typeset by Yorkhouse Typographic Ltd
Printed in Great Britain by Biddles Ltd,
Guildford and King's Lynn

CONTENTS

ACKNOWLEDGEMENTS

Grateful thanks for their professional help to: Michael Burton, partner at Brebner Allen and Trapp, Accountants; Andrew Belmont, senior partner at Vivien Stern Solicitors; Bhupinder Anand ACII ALIA (dipl.) MSFA, senior pensions consultant; and Sarah Killick and Fluffy O'Leary.

INTRODUCTION: WHY A GAY FINANCE GUIDE?

In the UK, there is a general reluctance for people to take financial advice from professionals. Most of us are happier to muddle along, dealing with our finances in a fairly *ad hoc* way. If we decide to buy a house, we trot off to the local bank or building society to arrange a mortgage. When the grey hairs begin to appear, we may start wondering how much money we will have when we retire.

The idea of making a proper financial plan probably never occurs to most people. And perhaps, for most people, there is no real need to worry. A big building society is no more likely to push you into a wildly risky home loan than a household name insurance company is to sell you a vastly inadequate pension. There is a minority for whom the fine tuning of their tax and investment affairs can have enormous benefits (and who are usually aware of their need for professional guidance), but most people's affairs are pretty straightforward.

For gay men the picture is very different. The attitude of the UK financial and legal establishment towards the HIV risk has, in recent years, turned gay finance into a minefield. Because a high number of personal finance products are based on life and health insurance, and because finance companies believe that discouraging gay clients is the way to avoid HIV related claims, it has become more difficult and more expensive than ever before for gay men to organize their finances. And this at a time when the UK gay community is safer than ever before, which only serves to compound the injustice.

Since the end of the 1980s, countless thousands have been denied life assurance, pensions, private healthcare, mortgages, and personal loans – all things the heterosexual community can acquire with ease. The good news is that things are changing. Even the most optimistic predictions from the Institute of Actuaries of the way HIV would spread during the 1990s are way off target. The worst scenario, of famine and financial ruin for all but the most cautious of insurance companies, now appears hysterical.

This, and the intense competition for business among UK insurers, has softened the former hard line against gay men taken by some companies, but many have not changed their stance. Choosing the wrong company could be disastrous. At best you could be charged 250 per cent more for a financial product than if you were heterosexual; at worst you could be blacklisted by the insurance industry and prevented from buying most types of finance products ever again.

This book is designed to help you overcome these problems. Each chapter discusses particular areas of personal finance, from making a will through taxes, mortgages, investment, and pensions, to health and life assurance. Each deals with the unique problems faced by gay men in making financial plans, and also describes the various products available.

The chapters can either be referred to as and when needed, or used together to help build a comprehensive financial plan. They are not ordered in a way that is intended to dictate the priority of everyone's financial plans. Personal circumstances vary a great deal. While for someone with dependants buying life assurance is probably the first and most important step, for someone nearing retirement the need to ensure the adequacy of their pension arrangements will be more pressing.

The first chapter, on wills and trusts, examines the special arrangements gay men should make to defend the financial interests of dependent partners when they die. Although writing a will is a precaution everyone should take, the reluctance of UK courts to recognize gay relationships means that gay couples should be doubly careful.

The Inland Revenue is, perhaps, less prejudicial towards gay people than other UK institutions. Heterosexuals and gays are fleeced of their earnings in fairly equal measure. But there are areas where gay people are either slightly worse off or where they enjoy a slight advantage. The chapter on taxation offers ways for gay men to reduce their tax bills, both while they are alive and – for the benefit of their dependants – after they die.

Mortgages pose particular problems for gay men. Securing a loan is often conditional on the borrower taking out life assurance; if the borrower dies before the loan is paid back, the lender will be reimbursed by the insurance company. Unfortunately, the life assurance industry's fear of HIV has made it impossible for many gay men to obtain either life assurance or a mortgage. Many have lied on application forms about their sexuality. This chapter describes how to raise a loan without lying, and outlines the various mortgages available. In some cases, as with pension mortgages, a home loan can deal with two areas of your personal financial plan in one go.

The investment chapter examines the various ways of saving money, from stuffing it under the mattress to wheeler-dealing on the stock market. Making money grow should be a central part of anyone's financial plans, but for gay men there are complications. Some of the most common types of investment include life cover, usually as a way of guaranteeing tax-free benefits. Because insurers fear HIV more than you do, any life cover may be offered to gay men only at an extortionate premium. These added costs can destroy the possible gains of some types of investment almost before they get started. Luckily, there are plenty of investment alternatives where the need for life assurance can be overcome.

Pensions are something we all need to plan for carefully. State benefits, already hardly adequate for most people, are fading year by year. But although all UK residents are encouraged to make their own provision for retirement, many pension plans are run by insurance companies. Once again this can be hugely problematic for gay men. The pensions chapter shows how to organize a pension without life assurance.

The private provision of healthcare is an emotive subject. But beyond sadness over the financial difficulties faced by the National Health Service is the realization by some people that only the private sector can help them properly if they become too ill to work. Unfortunately – again thanks to HIV – gay men have problems with health cover. Unlike life assurance, health insurance is easy enough to buy; it is when a claim is made that difficulties may arise. The chapter on health looks at the various types of health cover on the market, and the pitfalls gay men face with each one.

The chapter on life assurance deals with what is perhaps the most difficult area of gay finance. The appalling attitude of insurance companies to gay men is the main reason why the financial needs of gay men differ so much from those of heterosexuals. Even applying for life cover has to be approached cautiously.

Although the UK finance industry holds an exaggerated view of the way HIV is affecting the gay community, the danger for gay men remains a reality. Those who are HIV positive, whether they are gay or not, suffer an even more limited range of financial options. The last chapter examines the financial needs of HIV positive people and the various ways in which these needs might met.

An appendix provides information on where to go for professional financial advice, and how to complain if you feel the advice you are given is bad.

Readers in Scotland should note that in a few areas – such as trusts, and conveyancing for property transactions – the rules there differ from those in England and Wales. A good financial adviser will be able to help.

1

WILLS AND TRUSTS

One of the most frequently overlooked areas of financial planning is making arrangements for who gets what when one partner dies or if a relationship falls apart. For gay people it is especially important to consider how you would survive should either of these things happen to you. This chapter deals principally with the most basic provision anyone should make for their death – making a will – and also with trusts, another important means by which gay people can ensure that their assets are distributed after their death according to their wishes.

If your partner dies without making a will, even after a long relationship, you could have problems securing your portion of any shared assets. Apart from the obvious grief you would suffer, you could end up having an extremely painful and undignified scrap with your partner's relatives. The attitude of families towards a gay relative's partner often becomes hostile if the relative dies, especially where money is involved. This, more than the money, can be the hardest thing for bereaved partners to deal with. Worse still, with the law on their side hostile relatives will most likely win – perhaps leaving you homeless and broke.

The best thing to do is plan well in advance. Most people find the idea of dying a bit of a turn-off, so when you broach the subject with your partner try to use a little tact. Leaping straight into a discussion about how well off you'll be after he or she dies can lead to anything from slight nervousness to outright paranoia.

YOUR WILL

The single most effective thing you can do is to write a will, yet this is the one thing gay men and women most commonly overlook. It is a very simple and often cheap exercise and can save a whole lot of trouble. Anyone who dies without a will is said to be 'intestate'. This is a word with an appropriate history: in the days before we had the Bible, men who swore on oath did so with one hand cupped over their testicles – hence 'testimony'.

Dying intestate means that the County court will decide how your wealth will be divided according to strictly established rules. Your creditors will be paid first and your family second. Don't forget, though, that the law will not consider your gay partner a member of your family. One of my own clients whose partner failed to write a will lost the entire proceeds of his partner's insurance claim to a relative in Australia who, until then, he had no idea existed.

As long as the deceased was sane when the will was written and had complied with the necessary rules, the will is unlikely to be challenged successfully. There are, however, a few circumstances in which it can be. Only those who were financially dependent on you while you were alive could object if your death left them worse off and insufficient provision had been made for them in your will. In practice, such dependants will usually be relatives, but they can include gay partners.

While a will can theoretically be written on the back of an envelope, it should involve more than just scribbling down a few notes about who should have your money after you die. There are a number of rules laid down by the Wills Act 1837 that must be obeyed. The law was updated in 1982 to cut out some of the Act's outdated demands, but many wills are still invalidated by the courts every year because they have been written wrongly. Play safe and follow these basic rules:

- You must be over eighteen years old and of sound mind.

- The will must be written down – no clever parting shots on the camcorder.

- It must be signed by the person whose will it is (the testator).

- Two people must be present when the testator signs and must witness his or her signature by signing their own names underneath it. Neither witness can benefit from the will or be immediately related to the person making it.

DIY will-making

If you write a will yourself there is no need to wrap it up in the type of legalese a solicitor would use. Leave all the hereinafterwhereforeartthou's to the lawyers. (The wording they use is supposed to be unambiguous – even though most people do not understand it.) But though you can write your own will in plain English, it is still important to make sure there are no doubts about how you want your estate to be divided. Avoid using words that could be misunderstood or challenged. Writing something like, 'I want all my money to be shared between my family' should be avoided. Your idea of 'money' and 'family' could be very different to the court's.

Write exactly *what* you want to be given to *whom*, otherwise the court may decide not to allow the bequest at all. It will then become part of the residue of your estate and, unless there are alternative plans for it, will be divided under the intestacy rules.

If you are nervous about the legal wording of a will you can buy a basic will-form from many stationers. These contain a legally exact preamble together with a printed space for your last wishes and signatures from the testator and both witnesses. They also contain instructions on how the will-form should be completed.

Do this in a methodical way to ensure that no details are left out. First of all, make a list of everything you own. This should include all assets: money, property (including furniture), and anything else of value. Then draw up a list of your total debts: things like mortgages, loans, and overdrafts. Subtract the debts from the assets and you have the value of your estate before tax. For the tax year 1994/5, anything over £150,000 will be liable to inheritance tax (dealt with in Chapter 2). All money beyond the inheritance tax threshold is taxed at 40 per cent (see p. 28). Inheritance tax is payable where there is a transfer of value to another person, unless there is an exemption. In some circumstances, this tax may be payable on gifts made during your lifetime, although these are usually excluded if you survive for seven years after you've made the gift. Death, however, is always deemed to be a transfer of value and will therefore incur inheritance tax unless you are married. On death, the tax is levied at 40 per cent and is paid by the deceased's estate. When you have an idea of your net worth, draw up a list of the people you wish to pass it on to. Finally you simply take your will-form or a piece of paper and begin writing. Although the will can be written in your own hand, there is nothing to stop you using a typewriter. An added benefit is that a typewritten will is less likely to be open to misinterpretation.

If you are writing the preamble yourself and not using a will-form, you must word it carefully. It does not have to launch into the 'This is the last will and testament of [name] being of sound body and mind' you see in crime thrillers. But it is important to verify that it is indeed a will, and that it cancels all previous wills you may have written.

Begin by writing your full legal name. If all your friends call you something else, include the words 'sometimes known as [whatever]'. Follow this with a revocation of any other wills: 'I, [full name, address, and occupation], hereby revoke all previous wills and testamentary dispositions made by me and declare this to be my last will.'

The next line should state who the executor of the estate will be. This can be anyone you want – a professional executor if complicated trusts have been set up (see p. 28) – or perhaps the will's main beneficiary. Make sure, though, that the person you nominate is aware that you have done so and is willing to do the job. There should also be an alternative in case your first choice is not available when the estate comes to be settled. If a professional executor, such as a solicitor, is used you should include a sentence allowing him or her to bill your estate.

After this you list the beneficiaries. Exclude property such as houses and flats, which need a separate heading; this particular section deals with chattels and money. Start with chattels and say, 'I give the following specific legacies absolutely:', followed by a list matching each legacy to a beneficiary. Next, deal specifically with money. Start with

the clause, 'I give the following pecuniary legacies absolutely and free of all taxes:'. Then say which lucky devil gets
what.

It is possible to gift some of your estate before you die.
This is especially useful if your personal wealth looks like
exceeding the inheritance tax threshold (Chapter 2, on
taxation, deals with this more fully). One popular gift is the
Potentially Exempt Transfer. With PETs you can give away
anything you want tax free to whoever you want provided
you live for seven years after the gift is made.

Property

Property should have its own section. If you have been
cohabiting with your partner you will most likely want him
or her to inherit your share of the property. The property
may already be jointly owned by both of you, in which case
the surviving owner will probably inherit it. This may not
always happen: the deceased partner may, at some time in
his or her life, have committed an 'act of severance'. This is
simply a declaration that their interest in the property is
separate from your own and will be disposed of according
to the will.

Complications arise when one partner owns all of the
property or if both own it in equal shares. Writing a will
stating that you want the property to pass to your partner
may be sufficient in most cases, but not if you have a spouse
or a child hiding in the woodwork. For many gay people,
lurking husbands, wives, and children pose a particular
threat. Quite often people come out when they are older,
having tried to lead a heterosexual life. Because the law
doesn't allow them to marry their new partners, few bother
with a divorce. Others may have become involved in a

'marriage of convenience' with someone who wants to stay in the country.

While the relationship may be of no importance to the spouses themselves, the law will take it seriously. Under intestacy rules a surviving spouse is entitled to the first £150,000 of the dead person's estate if there are no children. If there are children, the spouse receives the first £150,000 plus a life share in half of what is left. The law may support the rights of the deceased person's spouse and children above that of a gay partner – even if none of them has ever lived in the property owned by the deceased and the partner. If the gay partner was being materially supported by the deceased at the time of death, a claim may be possible under the Inheritance Family Provisions Act. To avoid these complications you must specifically exclude the ex-spouse and state why a gift would be inappropriate.

This can all be avoided by drawing up a will or a trust document which sets forth the intentions of both partners following the death of either one (for trusts, see p. 18). The only way these can be challenged is if the person who makes the will or trust fails to make provision for a spouse or child who was financially dependent on the testator at the time of death.

In case the excitement of will-writing has tempted you into using jargonistic words like 'bequeath', you should be aware that, although you can bequeath chattels and money, you 'devise' property. The preamble of the property section should read: 'I devise and bequeath all my estate both real and personal whatsoever and wheresoever, subject to the payment of my debts and funeral expenses, to [partner's name] if he/she survives me by 28 clear days but if he/she should fail to survive me as aforesaid the succeeding provisions of this Will shall take effect.'

An important consideration with property is whether or not there might be any loans secured against it when you or your partner dies. It has to be made clear in the will how this debt is to be cleared up. With mortgages there is often a mortgage protection policy which on the borrower's death pays out an amount equivalent to the outstanding loan. Unfortunately the money is not automatically paid back to the lender: it will simply become part of the estate. So it is important to make it clear in your will exactly how you want the money spent. If the mortgage remains unpaid, it may have to be cleared from the residue of your estate, upsetting plans you had to make other gifts out of anything left.

The residue

A section of the will should account for the residue even if, by your calculations, your will disposes of everything. The period between your writing the will and your death will, you hope, be a long time. If it is, the estate may be worth much more than it was on the day the will was written. Unless some provision is made, any residue will be divided by the County court under the intestacy rules as though there had been no will in the first place. When dividing the residue, because it is going to be an unknown quantity, it is best to express each gift as a percentage. For example: 'Person A has 10 per cent of the residue, Person B has 15 per cent', and so on.

The final wording of the will has to include the signatures of the testator and of two witnesses. Above the testator's signature should be the words: 'In witness whereof I have hereunto set my hand this . . . day of . . . 19. . . Signed by the above named [testator's name] in our presence and then

by us in his [signature].' The witnesses should sign below
this, and print their full name, address, and occupation
underneath. Both witnesses must have actually seen the
testator sign, even though it is unnecessary for them to
know the contents of the will. Neither of the witnesses
can be a beneficiary of the will or the spouse of a
beneficiary.

Using solicitors

If you have any doubts about writing your own will, or if
your financial affairs are too complicated, it may be best to
employ a solicitor. This need not incur the huge costs
typically associated with legal work.

In recent years there has been a great deal of competition
among solicitors for business. Will-writing in particular is
one area where a little bargain-hunting can pay dividends.
Make a Will Week, promoted by the Law Society, looks like
becoming a regular event. This is a somewhat bizarre
occasion when otherwise staid solicitors dress up as a legal
superhero character called Will Power. If you can take a
lawyer seriously while he is wearing a leotard and tights,
this is the time to have your will drawn up. Firms may also
make promotional offers. During recent 'will-aid' weeks,
several insurance companies and banks have come up with
some cut-price deals. In one especially good deal, which
enabled you to make a will cheaply and donate to charity,
1700 solicitors offered their services free provided you gave
money to Oxfam, Christian Aid, or Save the Children. The
recommended donation was only £35 if the will was
straightforward. If it was more complicated a fee was
charged, but this applied only to a small proportion of the
wills made.

Even at normal rates, having a solicitor draw up a will can be relatively cheap. For most people, whose financial affairs are uncomplicated, the cost is around £75 plus VAT. Organizing a will for both you and your partner pushes the cost up to about £100 plus VAT. If your will is complicated in some way (because you have certain assets written in trust, for example – see p. 18), then the rate shoots up to a massive £100 per hour.

Finding the right solicitor can be less straightforward. Like all professions, the law has its share of bad apples. Any of the Law Society's 127 local branches will be happy to put you in touch with a solicitor, but sadly this is no guarantee that the solicitor is either competent or sympathetic to gay issues. It is much safer to trust personal recommendations. If possible, use someone you know to be both efficient and in tune with your needs. The Terrence Higgins Trust may be able to help; they run a legal telephone helpline (071-405 2381, Wednesday evenings, 7.00–9.00 p.m.).

Children

Where children are involved, wills need particular attention. Gay men and lesbians are increasingly becoming adoptive parents, sometimes as a result of one natural parent living with his or her partner. For gay men this situation often arises from an earlier heterosexual relationship – although cases of gay men successfully tackling the homophobic UK adoption process are not unknown.

The will should name a guardian. In heterosexual relationships this is to protect the child's interests only if both parents die. With many gay couples one of the partners is the child's actual parent, but guardianship may not automatically be granted to the person the child regards as its second parent if its actual parent dies. Make it clear in the will who the child's guardians should be in the event of the death of one or both partners. When children are adopted it may be necessary to change the will to include them. Even where provision has been made for 'all' your children – adopted or otherwise – only those who were adopted before the will was made will be taken to be included.

Having made these points it should be noted that gay parenthood is an extremely emotive issue in the UK. While it is important to include all the above information in your will, there is no guarantee that it will be carried out. The British legal system stoically refuses to recognize that gay people can be good parents. It is, therefore, impossible to be certain what will happen to a child following the death of a gay partner or even after separation.

Judges invariably conclude that a gay household is an improper environment for a child to grow up in. The question of child custody provides a salutary reminder of how little the attitudes of the British judiciary have changed – in spite of the opinion of some lawyers that progress is being made. Typical legal concerns are that a child brought up in a gay household will grow up gay, that it will be alienated from its heterosexual friends and embarrassed about its parents, or that it may be molested by its parents or parents' friends. All this in the face of overwhelming evidence to the contrary.

It would be over-optimistic to think that the courts will look favourably upon the type of security, welfare, and education a gay parent can offer a child. The majority of custody cases involve gay parents who had children before they came out, but the same difficulties, or worse, face gay couples who hope to adopt. As soon as a case comes to court, the custody battle invariably turns into a sordid voyeuristic circus. The outcome often hinges on who sleeps in which bedroom and who shares what bed. Other relatives, especially grandparents, may enter the picture and sometimes stand a better chance than the real parents of gaining custody.

As mentioned above, there are occasions when gay men and lesbians have been granted official custody of children, but this is far from typical. Where custody is granted it is often on condition that a gay parent separates from his or her lover. In judgments concerning heterosexuals, such a condition is enforced only if the child is in obvious physical danger. The child's wishes are unlikely to be considered. British courts are able to take a child's preference into account from the age of seven or eight in cases involving heterosexuals; in practice, court welfare officers usually take the child's wishes seriously after the age of ten. In custody cases involving gay men and lesbians, the court will mostly only consider the views of children if they are over fifteen or sixteen. Any younger, and it will be assumed the child was subject to some form of undue influence. The legal system will impose what it thinks is best for the child.

There was recently a change in the law. Now, under the new Children's Act, the wishes of the child must be considered more carefully than before. We have yet to see how this will work in practice.

Living wills

A growing number of cohabiting gay couples are organizing 'living wills'. These are similar to standard wills except that they state what medical treatment you would like to receive if you become too ill to make your thoughts known, instead of how you wish your estate to be divided upon your death. Under these circumstances, doctors normally turn to the patient's next of kin for advice. But because of the continuing failure of British law to recognize gay relationships, your partner would not automatically be consulted no matter how long you had been together. The spread of HIV has made living wills popular, but they can be used for any illness.

TRUSTS

Trusts can play an important part in the financial plans of gay people whether or not they are in a long-term relationship. Almost anything can be put in trust for the benefit of a third party. Trusts can be used in the same way as a will, to ensure that your estate is distributed in the way you want after you die. The main difference is that they can be activated by events other than death. This makes them an ideal vehicle for protecting a partner from possible hardship if the relationship breaks down. They can also help to relieve the possible tax burden on your partner or family after your death.

Although they are based on a very simple principle, the variety of trusts makes them hard to get to grips with. (They are also uniquely English. People looking into trusts in Scotland, for instance, will find they are very different from those south of the border.)

Broadly, there are two types of trust: private and charitable. Private trusts are, as the name suggests, intended to benefit individuals. The most common type is the 'express trust'. A will is a form of express trust. It is simply a way of stating your intentions in a given circumstance. There are three elements to it: the item in trust, the trustee, and the beneficiary. In the case of most individual trusts the trustee will be a solicitor.

Say, for example, that a couple shares a house but for some reason it must continue to be owned by one of them. It may suit them to have the property placed in trust for the benefit of whoever lives the longest. The solicitor effectively becomes the owner of the property, but is prevented from benefiting from it, and is empowered only to ensure that the property is transferred in accordance with the real owner's wishes. So when one or other of the partners dies, the solicitor will pass it on to the surviving partner.

As with wills, the wording of a trust document has to be precise. There has to be a specific intention. In the above example the intention is the transfer of your property when you die. There must also be a specific subject matter, in this case a particular property. Finally, there has to be an object: you have to state clearly who it is you want to benefit from the trust you are setting up. If any of these areas is unclear, the trust could fail.

The second type of individual trust is the 'implied trust'. These often arise out of confusion over how an express trust should be settled, and separate into two further types. A 'resulting trust' is based on the notion that, even when there are no specific instructions about how something in trust is to be treated, it is easy to work out what the intentions were. For example, you may have put something in trust for a partner or relative with the intention of giving them an income for life. If your partner dies the property and income will be held in trust for you, even though you have not expressly said it should be. In these circumstances, with both donor and beneficiary dead, the County Court will declare that benefits hitherto paid to the beneficiary will now go to the trustee.

A 'constructive trust' is usually the outcome of the intentions of an express trust having failed, or the trustee having been in breach of the trust. If, say, the wording of the trust was unclear, or events have overtaken its original aim, it is the job of the County Court to decide what the trust was set up to do. The same would be true if it were decided that the trustee had acted outside his or her remit. A court would then have to try to work out exactly what the intention had been, and impose its decision on the trustee.

Within these broad categories there are trusts for almost any conceivable event. Life interest trusts enable you to provide someone with a regular income for the rest of their life, following either death or the breakdown of your relationship. You could arrange this without necessarily giving up your ownership of whatever is in the trust. You could, for example, have a portfolio of shares held in trust from which a beneficiary would be paid an income from dividends (see Chapter 4). The shares themselves would still effectively be owned by you.

Discretionary trusts benefit one of a stated group of people. You could set up a discretionary trust which would, say, pay out a cash sum if a member of a particular group became too ill to work. The trustee's job, apart from holding the trust, would be to decide when the right circumstances applied and then make the payment.

Charitable trusts are typically set up for the relief of poverty or the advancement of education, and so are of little relevance in the realm of gay finance (unless you intend donating to one).

Trusts and tax planning

Trusts are also a useful tax planning vehicle. For the 1994/5 tax year the tax-free allowance on inherited money is £150,000. Those whose estate exceeds this value will lose 40 per cent of the surplus to the Exchequer. While it will make no difference to you personally, as by this time you will be dead, it could be devastating for your partner or dependants.

Because inheritance tax is based on the total worth of all your valuables, not simply the cash you have when you die, whoever inherits your estate may have to sell things off to meet the bill. This may not be too problematic if your estate is extremely large, but if it amounts only to the value of your property your partner or dependants may have to sell up to find the required cash. Once your net worth before inheritance tax exceeds the tax-free threshold, it is time to consider a trust. Anything held in trust for the benefit of someone else will not be included in the valuation of your estate.

Insurance trusts

The same protection can be given to insurance policies. Under UK law it is not possible for people who are not married to take out insurance on each other's lives unless an insurable interest can be proved. (Usually this occurs only in businesses where partners are financially interdependent.) For gay couples this causes particular problems. While a wife can be the beneficiary of a policy on her husband's life – or vice versa – partners in a gay relationship can only insure themselves. If you want your partner to receive the proceeds of the policy, you have to say so in your will.

Instead of insurance money passing directly to a gay partner when the policyholder dies, it becomes part of the estate. If the surviving partner has been catered for in the dead person's will the money may, of course, eventually get to where it was intended. But by then it could have been severely reduced by inheritance tax. If instead the policy has been held in an insurance trust, the policyholder can say exactly who is to have the money. This has two main benefits. First, there is money available for your partner immediately after your death; it will not be tied up in the often lengthy business of probate. Second, money from the policy will not be considered as part of your estate and will not, therefore, be liable to inheritance tax (of which more in Chapter 2).

Pension trusts

Pension trusts offer similar benefits, but with a different end in mind. Gay couples are often at a legal disadvantage when it comes to pensions. A heterosexual man's company pension or personal pension will include a widow's benefit: instead of his pension stopping completely if he dies, a reduced amount will be paid to his wife. In gay relationships the surviving partner receives nothing. A trust can do nothing about this if the pension is already being paid, but it can be used to protect your partner up until the day you retire.

If your pension is a money purchase scheme, your contributions will be invested in a fund, a proportion of which will be available as a tax-free lump sum and the balance available on retirement as an annuity (see Chapter 5). If you die before you are due to retire, the total fund value will be paid into your estate. To this extent the risks are the same as for insurance policies. The money will be tied up until your estate is sorted out, and by then it may have been hit by inheritance tax. With a pension trust you can place the fund outside your estate and nominate whoever you want to receive your pension rights instead. Once again, this means the money will be immediately available and free of all tax.

From ways of reducing tax liability when you die, we move on in the next chapter to look at how you can avoid paying money to the taxman while you are alive.

2
TAX

It's a very queer thing that, as far as the Inland Revenue is concerned, single people in relationships are not treated very differently from married couples. The only major downside is that on death gay partners may be liable for inheritance tax on what were jointly owned possessions. On the positive side, a partner's debts could easily die with them.

Tax is a cross we all have to bear. Most of us are taxed when we earn money, and taxed when we spend it. As Benjamin Franklin said, 'In this world nothing can be said to be certain, except death and taxes.' But by careful planning you can make sure that you pay not a penny more than you have to. For this reason, tax planning is an essential part of organizing your financial affairs.

By and large, gay people suffer the same problems here as any other taxpayers. Where there are differences these typically result in fewer benefits being extended to gay men than to heterosexuals. Of the three types of tax dealt with here – income tax, inheritance tax, and capital gains tax – it is inheritance tax planning which most often needs to be approached by gay men in a different way from heterosexuals.

As this point I should make a distinction between tax avoidance and tax evasion. Tax avoidance describes perfectly legitimate ways of reducing your tax bill. The Inland Revenue is never very happy about it, but there is nothing it can do other than to close any legal loopholes it feels are being abused. Tax evasion, on the other hand, is failure to pay the tax that you do owe. This is illegal. Staying on the right side of the law is essential when dealing with the taxman, even if the distinction between avoidance and evasion seems a little blurred at times.

As we shall see in Chapters 3, 4, and 7, on mortgages, investment, and life assurance, there are various financial products on the market offering tax-free benefits. Sometimes these can provide better homes for existing savings which are not being treated so favourably. But the main thing is to ensure that all your personal tax allowances are used to the full.

Personal allowances

Everyone in the UK is entitled to a number of tax-free allowances. There is no age limit on them. No matter how young or old you are, the same applies although the level of allowances varies. In some cases this has led people to set up trusts for their children to use their allowances. While this still goes on it is an area which anti tax avoidance rules have made increasingly tricky.

The personal tax-free earnings allowance is the same for anyone under the age of sixty-five in the UK. For the tax year 1994/5 this allowance is £3445. For those between sixty-five and seventy-four it is £4200, and for the over-seventy-fives it is £4370. Anything you earn above this amount in any one tax year will be taxed. One useful aspect of the tax-free allowance is that it is not divided between separate months or quarters of the year. If you were to work for just two months of the year, for example, and earn £3000, you would not be liable for tax. Although you might initially be taxed as if your earnings were going to be £1500 every month for the whole tax year, any money deducted can be claimed back. The amount of income tax you owe depends on your annual earnings.

INCOME TAX

For part of the 1980s and the early 1990s there were two tax bands: basic rate and higher rate. Basic rate taxpayers pay 25 per cent of taxable earnings to the Inland Revenue, while those on high incomes pay 40 per cent. In 1992 the government introduced a new rate of 20 per cent for those on lower incomes. So for the current tax year the first £3000 you earn above the £3445 personal tax allowance will be taxed at 20 per cent; for the next £17,255, up to £23,700, the rate increases to 25 per cent, and for earnings of over £23,700 above the personal allowance, income tax is 40 per cent.

Anyone who is employed is subject to Schedule E tax, more commonly referred to as pay-as-you-earn (PAYE). All of us are familiar with the way this works. Your company works out how much you owe and deducts it directly from your salary before you are paid. Almost anything your employer pays you, and most benefits in kind – like company cars, or cover for private medical expenses – are liable to income tax. Apart from your usual salary, any bonuses, commission, or money for meals or travel expenses covering your journey to and from work will be taxed as income.

The regime for self-employed people is a bit less harsh. There are numerous business expenses that can be offset against your tax bill. A few expenses can be similarly offset under PAYE, but it is up to you or your employer to prove to the Inland Revenue that such expenses were essential for you to do your work. If, for example, your job made it necessary for you to install a telephone in your home, you would only be able to offset it against PAYE if it were exclusively used for your work. This can be something of a grey area and is frequently challenged. Recently, a case came to court because of the Inland Revenue's refusal to allow people to claim relief against the cost of the journey from their home to their place of work. In some instances, as with doctors on house call or travelling salesmen, people have argued that they arrive at their workplaces as soon as they step outside their front doors. The Inland Revenue's usual response is that people who travel for a living, and are therefore entitled to tax relief for travel expenses incurred in the course of their jobs, are only deemed to be at their place of work after they have made their first call. One or two challenges to this ruling have been successful.

The self-employed are taxed under Schedule D. The complicated web of allowances and liabilities for those who work for themselves usually leads them to employ the services of an accountant. Sometimes, though, the amount of money they can legitimately chisel off your tax bill is cancelled out by the fees they charge. Other forms of income are sometimes taxed under different schedules and need to be declared on your annual tax return.

INHERITANCE TAX

One of the most neglected areas of taxation is inheritance tax planning. People quite often imagine it to be something affecting only the very rich. This may have been true at one time, but now more and more people find themselves lumbered with a huge tax bill after a partner or relative dies. The main reason for this is the rate at which personal wealth has outpaced the tax-free level for inherited money. For 1994/5, up to £150,000 can be left when you die without incurring a tax bill. Although this includes transfers made during a person's lifetime, most inheritance tax liabilities occur after someone has died. These days around 60 per cent of homes are owner-occupied, and in most cases the property will have been paid for by the time the owner dies. In spite of today's relatively static property values, a substantial proportion of properties are worth enough to take their owner's estate above the tax liability threshold after they die.

Even if the property's value is slightly below the tax-free threshold, the value of other items could push it over the top. Any cash, furniture, cars, curios, or other chattels we leave behind will form part of the Inland Revenue's arithmetic. Then comes the worst bit. Any part of your estate that exceeds the tax-free level will be taxed at 40 per cent. So, having worked hard to ensure the future security of your dependants, and despite having already paid taxes on a lot of the wealth you have accumulated, suddenly a huge proportion of it is lost to the government. This need not happen. With a certain amount of forward planning you can make sure that the people you leave behind gain the benefit of all or most of your estate.

Although the majority of tax problems have no special implications for gay people, inheritance tax is an exception. There are two areas in which gay people are at a disadvantage to heterosexuals. The first is that, within a marriage, the entire value of an estate can be transferred between the couple on the death of one of them without tax liability to the survivor; a tax liability can arise only on the death of the surviving partner. Gay couples do not enjoy this protection. If, for example, you share a £250,000 property which is fully owned by your partner, you will be hit with a massive bill if your partner's will passes ownership to you. The first £150,000 will be tax-free, the remaining £100,000 will be hit by £40,000 of tax. Unless you have that sort of cash handy to see off the taxman, the property will have to be sold to cover the cost and you will have to find somewhere cheaper to live. All the hard work and money the two of you put into building a home will be lost.

The second problem gay people face with inheritance tax planning is the perennial anti-gay attitude of UK insurance companies. For heterosexuals any tax bills on an estate that are known to be unavoidable can be anticipated with some form of life assurance policy. In the example quoted above, a policy paying out £40,000 to the surviving partner would prevent the property from having to be sold. When life assurance is available to gay men it is often at a hugely inflated price. The total premium cost over ten years or so could easily negate a large chunk of the tax saved by taking out the policy. But although tax planning through insurance is not out of the question (and is covered in more detail on p. 33), any other ways of mitigating against a future tax bill should be considered first.

Gifts

Because gay partners are not considered the legal equals of married heterosexual partners, it is impossible to pass – or 'gift' – your entire estate without incurring a tax bill on anything above the inheritance tax threshold. From a tax viewpoint, a gift occurs when assets are given away without the donor receiving cash or assets to the equivalent value in return. But there are circumstances under which tax-free gifts can be made. With property, it is important to make sure it is jointly owned and that full ownership will usually automatically pass to the surviving partner (see Chapter 1). This is straightforward enough if two partners buy a property together. For inheritance tax purposes, complications arise when the property is currently fully owned by just one partner. Simply giving your partner a legal share in the property is a non-exempt transfer of value, even if no actual cash has been transferred. So although the value of that portion of the property may not be large enough to cause an immediate tax liability, that portion will be offset against your inheritance tax allowance. So, although you may officially hand over a £100,000 share in the property to your partner, the Inland Revenue will continue to consider the (hoped-for) accumulating value of the gift to be part of the donor's estate.

There are ways round this. One is for your partner to buy half the property, and thus become legally entitled to the property after you die. The problem here is in the money you receive in payment, for it will form part of your estate and incur a tax bill after you die. It would be no use trying to sell your partner a share in the property for less than it is worth, either. A 'gain' (tax jargon for the increased value of assets) is not restricted to the actual cash you have received in return for your property, but is based entirely on the inherent value of the transfer. The fact that you have not received the full benefit of it will not be enough to deter the taxman. Alternatively, you can gradually transfer owner-ship by using up your smaller Annual Exempt Transfers, the several tax-free gifts the Inland Revenue allows all UK residents to make in a single tax year.

You can also provide gifts out of your regular income. However, this can be open to interpretation by your local tax office. For the gift to be exempt from tax, it must form part of 'normal' expenditure. In other words, the donor has to prove that he habitually gives money in this way. He should also be able to continue existing on the remaining income after such gifts are made. Gifts apparently forcing your earnings down to subsistence levels would not be allowed. You can also make an unlimited number of individual gifts under £250, either in cash or in kind. Any gifts made that are worth more than £250 will make you liable to tax on the whole amount at 40 per cent if you die, and not just the portion by which the £250 figure is exceeded.

Potentially exempt transfers

But more important than any of these for gay men in long-term relationships are Potentially Exempt Transfers (PETs). These allow you to gift as much of your estate as you want provided certain rules are adhered to. Such gifts can be made into some types of trust but, more importantly for gay partners, they can also be given to individuals.

The main stipulation is that the transfer is made no less than seven years before the donor dies. Quite clearly, this could pose a bit of a problem. Few of us can predict our demise with any degree of accuracy; certainly, few us would want it to happen purely for tax planning purposes. In fact the tax efficiency of this type of gift comes into play only three years after the gift is made, even though it will not be completely tax-free until after the full seven-year period.

The Inland Revenue operates a sliding scale of liability for PETs. If the donor dies within three years of a gift being

Number of years donor survives after making gift	0–3	3–4	4–5	5–6	6–7	7 or more
Percentage of gift liable to tax	100	80	60	40	20	0

Tapering tax relief for Potentially Exempt Transfers

made, the entire amount (subject, though, to the standard inheritance tax allowance) will be taxed at 40 per cent. As the number of years between the gift being made and the donor's death increases, the percentage of the gift liable to tax decreases, as shown in the table. This is known as tapering tax relief. Thanks to PETs, you can mitigate most or all of any future inheritance tax liability against the gradually decreasing risk of having all or part of a liability to pay.

Other tax-free gifts that can be made outside your partnership include the following: gifts to charities, gifts for a national purpose, gifts for the public benefit, gifts to political parties, and gifts to children in consideration of marriage. Gifts to charities are completely unlimited provided the charity is registered in the UK. The same is true for gifts for a national purpose; this includes money donated to art galleries and museums or colleges and universities. Gifts for the public benefit are pretty much the same, but cover a slightly broader range and include historic buildings or land. Because these gifts are less clear cut, it is best to clear each gift with the Treasury before going ahead with it. This is because your own idea of what is a gift for the public benefit may not be shared by the Inland Revenue. Gifts to political parties are restricted to those in the mainstream. Gifts in consideration of marriage will be of use to gay parents or gay couples who have legally adopted children. Each parent can gift £5000 to children who are about to marry, and each grandparent can also give £2500. You can also give £1000 to anyone who is about to marry, whether or not you are related to them.

Tax planning

These, then, are some of the measures you can take to reduce the risk of your estate being hit by inheritance tax demands. But there will be times when a bill is unavoidable, for example if the donor of a PET dies within the seven-year tapered relief period after a gift has been made. Although such bills may not be preventable, there are ways of making sure your estate is able to cope with them. The most common way of doing this is with the various forms of life cover (described in more detail in Chapter 7). A life policy will provide a lump sum after you die which can be used to pay an anticipated inheritance tax bill. For gay men this approach is only possible if they are insurable (see Chapter 7).

If cheap life cover is available to you, there are several different ways it can be used for inheritance tax planning, depending on your circumstances. The most common use for gay couples is as a way of covering the tapering liability of a PET gift. In some circumstances, to keep premiums at a minimum, the donor could buy a decreasing term assurance policy (see p. 177) covering the seven-year period of a possible liability. This would then be written in trust to the benefit of whoever is to receive all or part of your estate. Failure to do this would result in the proceeds of the life policy being considered as part of the estate and thus liable to a 40 per cent reduction. By keeping the proceeds separate from your estate, the full sum will be available for your dependants to offset against a tax bill. The sum assured under the decreasing term policy will be at its highest during the first three years after a PET gift has been made. From then on, as the possible liability reduces, so too does the amount of life cover the policy offers. Provided you are still alive at the end of the seven-year period, the policy and your tax liability for the original gift will expire together.

That may all seem straightforward enough, but there is a complication. PETs have a different priority from other parts of your estate when tax liability is calculated. For seven years after the gift is made, the full amount is considered by the Inland Revenue to form part of your estate. The gift also has first call on your £150,000 inheritance tax relief. If, for example, you were to die six and a half years after giving your partner a £100,000 PET and your estate is worth a further £150,000, you would expect that under the seven-year rule the Inland Revenue would take 20 per cent of £40,000, i.e. £8000. You might also expect that the remaining part of your estate, £150,000, would attract the full £150,000 inheritance tax relief, leaving your executors with no other tax bills to meet.

This would not happen as the PET is less than the level at which inheritance tax begins to be payable. The PET would have first call on the estate's full total £150,000 inheritance tax allowance, and would therefore be free of tax. Because the PET has already accounted for £100,000 of the inheritance tax allowance, only a further £50,000 from the rest of the estate can be passed on free of tax. Instead, £100,000 of your remaining estate would be taxed at the full 40 per cent, a disastrous £40,000. So in some cases the effect of using the PET route for making a gift will remain a liability on your estate at the full rate for seven years, even though you have officially given that portion away. The type of cover many people require is a level term assurance for the full seven-year period covering 40 per cent of the total value of their estate, including the value of any PETs, exceeding £150,000. The only difference between these and the example quoted above is that the amount of life cover you buy remains the same from the beginning of the term to the end.

Whole-of-life policies

Financial advisers are often keen to recommend a whole-of-life policy to do this job rather than a term assurance policy. As the name implies, whole-of-life policies remain in force for the rest of your life. With one of these you would still have life cover available even after any liability on the PET gift you make has expired. In some cases the premium is only slightly more expensive than for a term assurance policy. By having continuing life cover you could use it to cover any other liabilities. For example, your estate may have increased in value during the seven years following your original PET gift, and it may be necessary to reduce the value of your assets once more. An ongoing policy bought when you were seven years younger would certainly be cheaper than buying assurance afresh later on.

Ultimately it is up to you to decide which approach you prefer. Some people object to tax planning with life assurance in the first place, claiming that paying premiums over a period of years could cost more than the tax bill you are trying to avoid. But if the money which would otherwise be used to pay premiums is included as part of the total estate, that money will come into the calculation for inheritance tax liability.

Planning without life assurance

For a proportion of gay men, inheritance tax planning using assurance policies will be out of the question. You may be HIV positive, in which case insurance companies will consider you too high a risk. Even if you are not HIV positive, a suspicious underwriter may already have added your name to the Impaired Lives Register (see Chapter 7). But in many more cases gay men will simply balk at the unjustifiably high cost of insuring themselves and the attendant fuss and bother that making an application involves. However, in none of these circumstances does it necessarily follow that gay men should ignore inheritance tax planning.

As we shall see in Chapter 5 on pensions, it is possible to organize death-in-service benefits with a pension without taking out life assurance. If you die before you are due to retire, your estate will be paid either the total fund you have accrued to that date or the premiums plus interest. Approved occupational schemes are able to pay out up to four times the final salary (plus widow's benefits if applicable) you were due to receive plus your total contributions without creating any tax liability. This means that even if the value of your estate is over the £150,000 inheritance tax-free threshold, the death-in-service benefits paid by your pension will not form part of your taxable assets. Personal pension plans offer similar benefits. In this way the death benefits from either plan can be used to cover possible inheritance tax liability.

As with life assurance used for this purpose, it is essential for gay men to have such benefits protected under the terms of a trust or a will. Although death-in-service benefits will not form part of the total value of your estate, it is important to make sure they are directed to the person responsible for the tax bill on your estate. This is all the more important if the beneficiary of your estate is not the same person who will be looked after under the terms of your pension.

The only real shortfall in this arrangement is that it ceases to be of any use after you retire. As soon as you start taking the benefit of your pension, the death-in-service benefits lapse. Pension arrangements have become much more flexible during the last five years, and your retirement can now be delayed until you are seventy-five. But few people are in the luxurious position of being able to postpone taking their pension just to defend their death-in-service benefits. Once these benefits have disappeared, the only remaining way of planning your estate will be through life assurance.

If you now find this difficult and expensive – though not impossible – you will find it harder and more expensive as you grow older. The older you are, the shorter your life expectancy and the higher the insurance company's premiums. After the age of sixty-five, this is expensive enough for heterosexual men. Imagine what your premium will look like at this age after the insurance company has inflated it by 250 per cent to cover what it considers to be your high risk of contracting HIV. In all cases it is better to buy insurance when you are younger. A good adviser who is used to handling gay business will be able to take the sting out of dealing with insurance companies. For inheritance tax planning purposes, climbing the assurance hurdle now could pay huge dividends for your dependants later on.

CAPITAL GAINS TAX

Capital gains tax (CGT) is the third type of tax most of us need to be wary of. As with inheritance tax, we often fail to recognize situations where some kind of tax liability may have been created. With inheritance tax this is often the act of giving and receiving gifts (except where PET rules apply). For CGT it is anything which we can eventually swap for more money than we paid for it. Very often this applies to investments purposely made to create profits. Any regular payments you draw off such investments have to be declared for income tax purposes.

It is when all or part of the investment is disposed of that CGT becomes due. The amount you originally paid is deducted from the amount you finally receive, and the amount left is considered to be profit and subject to tax. The good news is that, like income tax, each UK citizen has an annual personal allowance. For 1994/5 this is £5800. The bad news for gay couples is that they do not enjoy the benefit of being able to transfer assets between each other free of CGT in the way that married heterosexual couples can. Any gains you make during the year have to be declared on your tax return. You then have until the end of the year (1 December) to pay any CGT you owe.

Like income tax, CGT can be offset against previous losses. Indexation will also help reduce your tax liability, as the purchase price can be nominally increased by the rate of the Retail Prices Index (RPI), which effectively gives you the gain in real terms on the sale and takes account of inflation. Capital losses you make this year can be carried forward and added to your tax-free allowance for next year. The rate at which you are taxed for capital gains depends on your prevailing income tax rate. The net amount of capital gains that is taxable after all allowances have been made is added to your income tax bill in the year it falls due. This, more than anything, underlines the need to be careful about when you dispose of assets. If, for example, your earnings currently fall slightly short of the 40 per cent higher rate tax band, the addition of capital gains may (temporarily) push you over the limit. The portion by which your capital gains overshoot the 25 per cent basic rate tax level will, therefore, incur a 40 per cent tax charge. If this is likely to happen you should, if possible, think about staggering the amount of assets you dispose of. Investors often choose to do this at the end of one tax year and the beginning of the next. By dividing the asset disposal over the two days where two tax years meet you will enjoy the benefit of two lots of tax-free allowances.

Many investors who might not otherwise be thinking of disposing of their assets frequently plan well in advance as a way of mitigating future CGT liability. One very popular way of doing this is called 'bed and breakfasting'. As a way of gradually reducing the overall tax liability of an appreciating asset, the owner will sell all or part of it at the end of the tax year in order to benefit from any of the £5800 tax-free allowance that remains unused. Having mopped up the allowance in this way, the investor usually buys the asset back again.

Outside the investment market, for most people the one appreciating asset is their home. For most of the 1980s the gains homeowners enjoyed were phenomenal. While such madcap gains are unlikely to recur during the 1990s, it is important to be aware of any capital gains liabilities arising out of increasing property values. In the majority of house sales no liability is incurred because all profits made from your principal residence are exempt from tax. But there are occasions when homeowners may find themselves faced with a large tax bill. Problems can easily arise where there is some doubt over the definition of residence. Residence for most homeowners is the property they own, but there are some people who do not live in the property they have bought.

This applies to homeowners caught in the negative equity trap – where the property's value has dropped below the amount the mortgage lender is owed. Those who have to move to another area but cannot sell their property may be forced to let it and rent another property for themselves. Any gains made on the property during the years the owner does not live in it could be taxable. The good news is that negative equity is allowable against tax.

Complications may also arise if the property is not used exclusively as a private residence. If you work from home, either full-time or part-time, you can usually take advantage of certain tax allowances for any facilities you use for your work. You can claim relief for a room used solely as an office, plus a portion of your heating and lighting bills, as business expenditure. This is all very useful when it comes to reducing your annual tax bill, but it may compromise your ability to claim all future gains on the property tax free. Luckily it is rare for people to lose exemption for this reason unless the building was used exclusively for business. Also, countless homeowners have unknowingly avoided a tax bill simply because they were unaware that there might be a liability.

The question of principal residence can also come under scrutiny where you help a third party to buy a property. This happens most commonly within families, but applies equally to such arrangements between friends. The following example is typical. Person A decides to buy a property. Unfortunately his earnings and savings are not sufficient for him to raise enough capital. Luckily, he has person B to help him. B has plenty of equity within his own property and has enough earning power to raise further capital against it. He can either borrow the money himself against his own property for A to use, or can enter into a joint mortgage with A which is secured against the property A intends to buy. Whichever arrangement they enter into, the following could happen. For mathematical convenience, let's imagine that A and B have equal shares in A's property. This year the property is worth £60,000, and each of them owes £30,000. In five years' time A decides to sell up, and the property is worth £100,000. When B pays off his outstanding loan he is £20,000 better off. If we assume that CGT allowances are the same as they are now, and that B has no other CGT liabilities, only the £5800 tax-free allowance plus indexation benefit of this profit can be taken tax-free. (The purchase price is indexed to the RPI, which reduces the gain on sale by artificially inflating the original cost.) If the value of the property grew at the same rate as the RPI (or less), no CGT will be owed. Anything outside these allowances will be charged at B's standard tax rate as though it were income earned in that year. The same applies to holiday homes or other second homes in the UK or abroad and owned by UK taxpayers, regardless of whether or not they are used for business.

Apart from residential property, there is a range of other appreciating assets that are exempt from CGT. Individual chattels worth less than £6000 are not liable, neither is foreign currency forming part of your personal expenditure outside the UK. On the investment side, National Savings Certificates are exempt.

There are, of course, various tax-free savings plans (discussed in Chapter 4) which also carry no capital gains liability: Personal Equity Plans and Enterprise Investment Schemes, for example. Profits from the ownership of woodland or cars are also free of CGT. This latter exemption has proved extremely beneficial for those lucky enough to cash in on the boom in classic car values a few years ago. Some non-exempt assets may avoid capital gains liability if they are disposed of in a particular way. Works of art acquired by the Inland Revenue as an in-kind payment of inheritance tax liability will not attract CGT liability. Gifts to charities or housing associations are also exempt.

Finally, there are a number of windfall benefits which the Inland Revenue cannot get its hands on. If you are a bigtime punter at the racetrack, your winnings are subject to gaming tax if you have not already paid this tax on your stake, but are wholly exempt from CGT. Unfortunately, this does not extend to claims paid by insurance companies, especially on property, unless the insurance covers an exempt asset such as your main residence. In other circumstances – where jewellery is stolen, for example – a subsequent payment from an insurance company will be liable to CGT in the same way as if the asset had been disposed of on the open market. The same is true where property other than your main residence is acquired under a compulsory purchase order. Any profits made on the deal, whether you were a willing party or not, will be liable to CGT. Any medals you have received for bravery can be sold at a taxfree profit too. The main proviso here is that they can be sold only by the person who received the award. Profits made by those who buy and sell medals are taxable in the normal way.

• TAX •

Having looked at, among other things, the disposal of a
property, we now examine what is involved in buying one –
in particular, the various types of mortgage available.

3

MORTGAGES

In personal finance terms, mortgages are relatively straight-forward. A mortgage lender will give you some or all of the money to buy a property provided you can afford the repayments and the property is worth the amount you intend paying for it.

For gay men this simple transaction can become very complicated. The problems begin when a lender makes one of two possible demands. First, they may insist that the loan is secured with a life assurance policy in the borrower's name with all benefits assigned to the lender. Should the borrower die while the loan is outstanding, the proceeds of the policy will be paid directly to the bank, building society, or finance house making the loan.

Second, with some types of loan you are required to buy an endowment policy. (This is explained in more detail on p. 56, but is basically a way of ensuring that the full amount borrowed is available to be paid back at the end of the mortgage term.) The problem for gay men is that endowments are based on life assurance, and that the insurer will most likely consider you a prime HIV risk as soon as your sexuality is made clear (see Chapter 7). But even if you are offered cover, having suffered the trauma of an HIV test and the insurance company prying into your private life, you will probably be charged an extortionately high premium.

Should I lie?

To avoid these problems, hundreds of gay men have lied about their sexuality on insurance company proposal forms. The trouble is, this could create more difficulties for gay borrowers than for the insurance companies. If you are found to have lied on a proposal form, the insurer will most likely refuse to pay up if you die before the term of the policy. The company will probably also hang on to all the premiums you have paid in. At best your estate would receive a portion of the premiums minus some stiff administration charges. The lender will then repossess the property and sell it to recoup the money outstanding; if there is no immediate sale, regular interest charges will be added to the amount outstanding and deducted from any eventual profit on the property which would otherwise have gone to any dependants you may have.

The saddest part is that this is all unnecessary. An independent financial adviser who is used to dealing with gay finance will know which lenders are more flexible about life assurance. Although lenders have nearly always demanded you have either a term assurance or an endowment policy before they grant a mortgage, things are changing. This is partly because of pressure from the gay community, and partly because of competition in the mortgage market. Lenders are increasingly realizing that the real security they have is in the worth of the property. Provided they value it sensibly, they have little chance of losing out on any deal. Their only risk is if the property is destroyed by fire or explosion, or if it slips inelegantly into a hole in the ground. All these risks can be covered with a relatively cheap property insurance (see p. 69).

Raising a mortgage

Apart from the value of the property itself, your own financial position will obviously have a bearing on whether or not anyone wants to lend you the money. And, bearing in mind the problems many borrowers have suffered since the UK property market tumbled after 1988, it is equally important for those considering a mortgage to make sure they can cover the cost. The most obvious point to consider is whether you can afford the regular mortgage repayments.

Most lenders will offer a maximum advance based on a multiple of the borrower's salary, usually 3. If your gross annual salary is £25,000, therefore, you can raise a mortgage of £75,000. When two people are buying a property together, both their incomes are added and then multiplied by (usually) 2.5 to give the total mortgage advance. To continue with the above example, if the second borrower earned £20,000 the maximum advance would grow to £112,000. (Occasionally the second borrower's income is merely added to the total advance, which in this example would give a maximum advance of £95,000.) If more than two people want to buy a property jointly, most lenders will offer an income multiple based on the salaries of all the prospective borrowers. Lenders' criteria differ greatly; examples of formulae for three borrowers are 3 times the highest income plus 1 times the other two, or 2.5 times two incomes plus 1 times the other.

Apart from the cost of mortgage repayments anyone buying a house will have to cover a range of other expenses. These include stamp duty, the local authority search fee (to make sure there are no plans to put a motorway through the building), a structural survey, the Land Registry fee, and solicitor's fees. Here is a case study based on the purchase of a property in outer London for £100,000:

- *Stamp duty.* 1 per cent of the entire value of property costing more than £60,000: £1000.

- *Search fee.* Varies between local authorities, but typically: £85.

- *Survey.* There are three types: a lender's survey, to ensure property is worth the amount paid for it, about £150; a 'home buyer's survey' by the lender, which is more extensive, about £250; or a full structural survey by an independent surveyor, £250–£500 + VAT. In this case the borrower opts for the lender's survey: £150.

- *Land Registry fee.* Varies; say £150.

- *Solicitor.* Typically £325 + VAT at 17.5 per cent (£57): £382.

- *Total cost*: £1767.

If you are also selling a property there will be further costs. Estate agency fees typically range anywhere from 1 to 3 per cent of the purchase price, depending on whether or not you have one or more agents trying to sell your property. There will also be further solicitors' fees of around £325 + VAT, again for a house costing £100,000. You may also need to hire the services of a removal company. Costs vary widely, depending largely on the distance from A to B, but a ball-park figure is £500 + VAT.

The good news about the cost of a mortgage is that £30,000 of the amount borrowed attracts tax relief – at 20 per cent for the 1994/5 tax year. This is deducted automatically from each repayment under a system called Mortgage Interest Relief At Source (MIRAS). A loan of £50,000 may, for example, cost £500 a month. The first £30,000 costs £300, which the relief reduces to £255, so the amount

you actually pay would be £455. The bad news is that
MIRAS is being phased out. The £30,000 limit has
remained unchanged – even during periods when the
average mortgage size increased – and successive budgets
have reduced the amount of tax relief available. On current
plans, MIRAS will be phased out, falling to 15 per cent in
1995/6 and disappearing by 1998/9.

From being a very complex business years ago, raising
a mortgage became much easier during the 1980s. But
because so many lenders have accumulated bad mortgage
debts, the trend is towards a much closer scrutiny of
prospective borrowers' credentials. Gone are the ludicrous
income ratios of four times primary income plus three times
the second income that at least one lender offered at the
height of the mortgage boom. To prove that you earn
enough you will be expected to provide wage slips. Your
salary will be verified on the loan application form by a
signature from your boss or accountant. Bank references,
landlords' or previous lenders' references, and employment
history are often asked for.

Since the property slump, some companies have dispensed entirely with standard income ratios. The weakness
of these ratios is that although they prove how much you
earn, they give absolutely no indication of how much you
spend. While loan application forms ask you for details of
any other outstanding loans, they fail to go any further. A
few lenders now require an affordability statement with
the main application, in which you have to declare all your
earnings plus all your regular living expenses. By subtract-
ing one from the other the lender arrives at a net disposable
income. If the expected monthly repayment costs exceed a
set percentage of your available disposable income, your
application for a loan will be declined. Under this stricter

regime some lenders are claiming to be turning away half the mortgage applications they receive. The reason this practice has not become more widespread is that some lenders are worried that such an intrusive and complicated application process will deter good business as well as bad.

All mortgage advertisements now carry a 'financial health warning', which is worth repeating here. Remember that your home is at risk if you fail to keep up the repayments on your mortgage or any other loans you have secured against your property.

The self-employed

The self-employed must demonstrate their income by presenting their accounts, usually for at least the previous three years. Those without enough of a trading history could have problems unless they find one of the rare lenders prepared to take an accountant's word about their current earnings and future potential. Being self-employed can be a particular problem if an accountant has successfully whittled down his client's tax bill by offsetting various expenses against it. While this is useful for tax saving, it does make earnings appear low on paper. Many self-employed business people who proudly boast of paying hardly any tax are incredulous at the attitude of most lenders to their 'official' earnings, but they should really not be so surprised. Their best hope is to put their hefty tax savings aside for a deposit on a property.

Non-status mortgages

By building up a large enough deposit, you could become eligible for a non-status loan. As with all loans, their availability depends largely on current market conditions.

Unlike the position with more basic mortgages, non-status lenders demand no proof of your ability to repay the loan. The catch is that they usually demand a deposit of at least 25 per cent of the property's value, and usually 30 per cent. Some lenders will ask you to prove where the money came from – a bit tricky if you robbed a bank or got away with a massive tax fraud. The lender's lack of concern about the amount you earn to repay this type of loan is based on two factors. First, it is taking a 30 per cent lower risk than with, say, a 100 per cent loan. If you fall into arrears the property will be repossessed and sold before the lender's 70 per cent stake in it is breached. Second, most people are unlikely to put 30 per cent of their own cash into something if they think they have no chance of paying off the loan.

The availability of different types of mortgage depends on market conditions. If lenders are cash-rich they may make 95 per cent or 100 per cent loans available. In more difficult times people buying property will have to put together a larger deposit. This is often easier for those who are already some way up the property ladder. When they sell their current property there may be money left over after the mortgage has been repaid, and this 'equity' can then be put towards the cost of the new property.

First-time buyers will have to find a deposit some other way. Lenders and insurance companies occasionally have savings schemes specifically geared to house purchase. After saving a set amount with them for a specific period, a loan may be available on preferential terms.

Indemnity policies

A lender prepared to lend more than 75 per cent of the value of a property will usually demand the one-off payment of an indemnity insurance premium. Your ability to buy this type of cover is unaffected by sexuality. Indemnity insurance comes into play if a property is repossessed. If lenders are unable to recoup all of the money owed them, insurers will make up the difference. Lenders began insisting on this type of cover after some of them had their fingers burned in the 1980s with 100 per cent loans. Some borrowers even moved into a property but never made any repayments. It might be six months or more before the property was repossessed. The repayment arrears would be added to the amount the lender was owed, but unless the property had increased substantially in value during that time, the lender would lose money when the property was sold.

But the property slump of the late 1980s exposed a nasty side to indemnity cover. Very few lenders bothered to explain the exact workings of this type of cover, except to say that it protects advances over 75 per cent of the property value. Not surprisingly, borrowers assumed that because they were paying the premium it was they who were insured. Not so – it is the lender that is insured, not the borrower. If the borrower defaults on the mortgage and the lender is subsequently out of pocket, the lender will make a claim against the insurer under the terms of the indemnity agreement. The insurance company, as promised, will pay for any losses the lender incurs on loans above 75 per cent of the property's value. So far so good, but the indemnity insurer might then sue the borrower in a bid to retrieve the money it paid out.

This was a huge shock for many of those unfortunate enough to have their homes repossessed after the property slump. Having extricated themselves from the burden of a mortgage they could no longer afford on a property which was often worth less than they bought it for, they hoped their nightmare was over. It was not. On top of losing huge sums of money and their homes, they found themselves facing legal action and a demand for thousands of pounds. This might not seem such a glaring injustice had the borrowers not paid the insurance in the first place. Imagine the fuss if it happened with any other type of insurance. You pay an insurance premium on your car, say, and you make a claim because it is stolen. The insurance company sends you a cheque and then threatens legal action to get it back. With indemnity insurance, it seems, insurers get their cake and get to eat it too. The worst aspect of all this is that it affects those who are least able to pay.

Although not all indemnity insurers are mean-minded enough to sue, they have generally shown an increasing enthusiasm to do so. This is mainly because of the financial problems that beset insurance companies during the most recent recession. While the property market was booming, the indemnity insurance was a nice little earner for mortgage lenders and insurance companies. The insurance company took the premium on what it considered to be low- or no-risk business, out of which the lender took a fat commission. The property slump caught everyone unawares, and indemnity claims rocketed. Insurance companies, especially, hardly imagined that the halcyon days of the property boom would end. The premiums they had collected proved hopelessly inadequate for plugging the hole indemnity claims made in their profits. Menacing borrowers for their money back was the only way some of them could recoup their losses.

Unfortunately, being aware of this injustice will not prevent it happening. Lenders of advances above 75 per cent of the property's value will continue to demand indemnity premiums, and borrowers have to stump up the money or face missing out on buying the property they want. Following the recent experience of insurers in the indemnity market, indemnity insurance is generally becoming much more expensive than it used to be. The important thing is to bear in mind who will be protected by the insurance if things go wrong in the future.

What is more frustrating for home buyers is that indemnity insurers have now increased premiums on all new policies to make up for the money they lost during the 1980s through their lack of foresight. Premiums are now between 4.5 per cent and 7 per cent of the amount insured. In some cases this can be the largest lump-sum cost a borrower incurs. Yet, ironically, the claims risk of those buying indemnity cover now is much lower than it was during the 1980s when policies were cheaper. Properties are now being bought at the bottom of the market.

Which mortgage?

The range of different types of mortgage grew incredibly during the 1980s thanks to financial deregulation. Competition hotted up when insurance companies and financial institutions other than banks and building societies began lending money for buying property. Various lenders tried different ways of getting one up on the opposition.

The more radical changes in the mortgage market were forced by the centralized lenders that sprang up during the 1980s, such as the Home Loans Corporation and National Home Loans. Unlike traditional lenders they have no branch networks. Instead, loans are made through financial advisers or insurance companies that use mortgage business as a way of generating commission income on various attendant insurance policies. Their overheads are generally lower than those of banks and building societies, and originally they were not constrained by the same financial regulations. In particular, they were permitted to raise a higher proportion of cash on the money markets and were not limited by the need to attract deposits from savers. As a result, they were often able to lend money at highly competitive rates.

To break into what was a highly traditional and fairly stuffy market, the centralized lenders began attaching various marketing 'bells and whistles', such as fixed-interest loans and various 'cheap' starter mortgages for first-time buyers. Many of these have been adopted by the traditional lenders. To this extent, borrowers owe a debt of gratitude to the centralized lenders. But for those thinking of using a centralized lender, a certain amount of caution is required. When the property market turned sour in the late 1980s, many of these brash new players were caught on the hop. Several of them decided to abandon the market altogether, but not before they had clobbered borrowers by jacking up interest rates. When building society interest rates were at their highest, many borrowers with centralized lenders were paying 3 to 4 per cent above the average. Some centralized lenders also resorted to increasing interest rates to well above the average on fixed-rate and first-time-buyer mortgages once the term of the tempting 'special offers' expired.

Under normal circumstances, a borrower in this position would be able to remortgage the loan with another, cheaper lender. Unfortunately the fine print of some mortgages offered by centralized lenders made this almost impossible. Borrowers wanting to pay off their mortgage early would have been hit by enormous penalty charges. Finally they had only two unsatisfactory options: to live with the inordinately high interest rates for as long as possible, or to fall into arrears and face repossession.

In fact, early redemption penalties, as lenders describe them, are widely used, in most cases as a threat to prevent borrowers being tempted away by cheaper lenders. Even so, redemption penalties are rarely so high as to make it financially impossible for borrowers to change lender if they really want to. A typical penalty clause would stipulate that if the mortgage is redeemed within the first two to five years of the loan being made, the borrower will be charged three to six months' extra interest. If you redeem your mortgage early because you are buying another property, the lender will usually waive all penalties provided you take out your next mortgage with them, but some do not.

TYPES OF MORTGAGE

Exactly which type of loan you opt for depends on your particular needs. Some types are more appropriate to gay men than others.

Repayment mortgage

The repayment mortgage is the bog standard, no-nonsense home loan. The lender pays you an advance and you repay the loan at regular intervals over a specified term – usually 25 years. Each regular repayment is made up of interest on the loan plus a portion of the loan itself. In the early days of the mortgage, each repayment is mostly interest with only a tiny portion of capital. This balance gradually changes over the term until, towards the end, most of each repayment is capital and only a small part is interest. In this way the amount you owe gradually reduces over time.

Repayment mortgages became less popular with the arrival of new and flashier home loans. Now, though, they are enjoying something of a renaissance following some of the bad experiences people have had with other types of mortgage. More of that later.

For gay men, the problem with repayment mortgages is that lenders expect the loan to be covered by some form of life assurance, usually a decreasing term policy. With such a policy, the amount of life cover gradually reduces over the period of the mortgage, and should mirror the amount of money owed to the lender at any one time. If the borrower dies, the policy will pay off whatever is left of the mortgage. Should you find obtaining life cover a problem, ask an independent adviser whether there are lenders currently making loans that are not conditional on buying life cover.

While journalists may harp on about how good repayment mortgages are, they are less appropriate for gay men and lesbians, who tend to move home more often than heterosexuals, perhaps as often as every five years. Whenever you move you will have to start another 25-year mortgage, and will be continually hit by the heavy interest payments of the early years.

Endowment mortgages

This is the most popular type of mortgage, and accounts for roughly 70 per cent of the total mortgage market. It first became popular during the early 1980s. There are two elements to it: one is the loan, and the other is an endowment policy from an insurance company. Endowment mortgages are often cheaper than repayment mortgages, and no matter how many times you move there is no need to keep renewing the term of the loan. This is because the endowment that will eventually pay back the loan can be transferred between mortgages. If your new mortgage is bigger than the last, you should be able to increase the value of the endowment without starting a new one. Otherwise it may be necessary to buy another endowment to run along-side the existing one by way of a top-up. The lender issues an advance for a specified time in much the same way as with a repayment mortgage. The difference is that, instead of gradually paying back the capital, all you repay at intervals is the loan interest; at the same time, though, you make regular investments in an endowment policy assigned to the lender. This has two functions: first, it insures the lender against your dying while you still owe it money; and second, the value of the policy grows until, at the end of the term, it should pay out a sum at least equal to the original advance. Unfortunately, there is no guarantee that it will. While endowment policies are less risky than some other forms of investment, the amount they return does depend on how well the company manages its clients' money.

This type of package was first sold by lenders and insur-ance companies on the back of three benefits. The first was the availability of MIRAS tax relief on 100 per cent of each repayment to the lender for the first £30,000 of the loan. The second was that the premium on the endowment policy was subject to Life Assurance Premium Relief (LAPR), even though only a small part of it was used to buy life cover. Although LAPR was abolished in 1984, endowment policies from before then still attract tax relief (albeit at the much reduced rate of 12.5 per cent of the total premium).

Apart from the portability of endowments from one loan to another, the remaining benefit – and one which continued to apply even after the other tax benefits on endowment mortgages were heavily reduced – is that the cash sum eventually paid out by the endowment policy is tax free. If the policy performed as well as planned, there would be a lump sum available even after the mortgage had been repaid. Those selling endowment mortgages usually claimed there could be no doubt that the money the policy would pay out would be more than the amount owed to the building society. Usually they told borrowers that it would be a good deal more. However, since the stock market crash in October 1987 insurance funds have struggled to maintain their investment performance, and it has become harder for insurance companies to continue paying out record levels of bonuses to endowment policyholders. Although there have been no instances of companies failing to return the amounts needed to pay off home loans, it is wisest to opt for the better-known insurance companies. If you have any doubts, ask an independent financial adviser.

For gay men, an additional problem is the life insurance element of endowment mortgages. Unless you have an existing endowment policy predating the HIV paranoia of the insurance industry, it may be better to choose another type of mortgage. But endowment insurance can be easier to buy than pure life assurance because companies greedy for the large commissions they can levy on bigger premiums may be less stringent about medical questions.

PEP mortgages

PEP mortgages are similar to endowment mortgages in that the monthly repayments are divided into two parts: interest on the loan and a regular contribution to a savings plan which will eventually be used to repay the lender. With

PEP mortgages the savings element consists of a Personal Equity Plan – a government scheme offering tax advantages to people investing in the stock market (see Chapter 4). The tax advantages offered by PEPs and the chance of enjoying any stock market gains during the term of the mortgage are making them increasingly popular. Those using them hope that their PEP will grow faster than an endowment policy would. This would give them the option of either paying off the mortgage early – thus cutting the number of years for which interest has to be paid – or receiving a larger tax-free sum in excess of the amount needed to repay the loan at the end of the mortgage term. An important consideration here is the risk attached to a PEP investment. The volatility of the stock market could just as easily produce a painful loss. A stock market crash just before you planned on cashing the plan in could leave you short of the amount needed to pay off the loan. There is also the political risk that a new chancellor might abolish them. While this might not affect existing PEPs, the growth of any further savings in the ex-PEP mortgage could attract a tax bill.

PEP enthusiasts rarely understand why anyone would ignore the tax benefits of a PEP by organizing a mortgage any other way. But there are circumstances in which the PEP route is unsuitable. To begin with, the borrower may have other plans for his or her annual PEP allowance. In spite of the tax advantages, there are one or two things to be wary of. Higher than average charges with PEPs mean that where relatively small amounts are invested costs can work out disproportionately high and destroy any would-be tax benefits. This is certainly more likely for basic-rate than for higher-rate taxpayers.

PEP mortgages do represent less of a commitment than other types of repayment vehicle as the fund can be cashed in at any time, unlike a pension mortgage fund (see p. 61), and any proceeds will be tax-free, regardless of how long the policy has been held. Also segments of the contract can be cashed in without having to encash the entire fund. The major disadvantage of doing this is that you may find that you have dipped into the fund so often that you are left with insufficient funds to pay off the mortgage.

PEPs are also sold on an annual basis, which makes it impossible to buy a PEP for a 25-year term, for example. If the government gets bored with them halfway through your mortgage term, you will have to find another way of building a fund to pay back your lender.

All the same, if you are happy with the possible pitfalls you should go for it, especially if you are a higher-rate tax-payer. Remember, though, that some lenders will insist on you buying life cover as part of the PEP mortgage package, which brings us back to the same old insurance problems.

Unit trust and investment trust mortgages

Some borrowers may prefer to use unit trusts or investment trusts to run alongside their mortgage. These operate in a similar way to endowment and PEP mortgages, except the money that will eventually pay back the loan is saved in either a unit trust or an investment trust (see Chapter 4). As with other types of mortgage, these can be arranged through most lenders or financial advisers.

Pension mortgages

Pension mortgages provide another way of building up tax-free benefits to pay off an interest-only loan. Commonly known as Section 226 policies (see p. 113) in the days before personal pension plans arrived, they were mainly used by self-employed or non-pensionable people who, at that time, were the only individuals in the UK allowed to buy private pensions. Since the extension of individual private pensions to all UK residents in 1988, this option has become more widely available.

Those paying into a personal pension can take up to 25 per cent of their total fund on retirement as a tax-free lump sum, excluding the protected rights proportion of the fund. Protected rights are the equivalent of your state pension benefits funded by your NI contributions. By running a personal pension alongside a mortgage, part or all of this money can be used to repay the loan. This can be extremely cost effective. Depending on your age, the percentage of net relevant earnings (your total taxable income) that can be paid tax-free into a personal pension is from 17.5 per cent to 40 per cent (see p. 119). All income and capital gains on the pension fund itself are also free of tax.

For gay men there are particular advantages and disadvantages to this arrangement. The main disadvantage is that many personal pensions are packaged with life assurance, which is both unnecessary and presents obvious complications. The long and the short of it is that pension mortgages are the most flexible, tax efficient way of paying a mortgage. Unless you belong to a company pension scheme, they are well worth considering. For gay men the best thing about pension mortgages is that they are a way of overcoming the fear that can be associated with making provision for retirement. Many are afraid of their HIV status, or punch-drunk from the number of friends dying of Aids. This all makes it hard to plan for a retirement which some fear they will never reach. With a pension mortgage, the repayment of the loan can be seen as the most important factor and the pension itself a bonus.

The government does not recognize the existence of pension mortgages. For this reason personal pensions cannot be assigned to a lender in the way that endowment policies can, so it is impossible for a lender officially to have first call on your pension lump sum. Instead, the lender has to trust that you will pay the mortgage back when the time comes.

The main consideration is how well a pension mortgage would fit in with your general financial plan. You should consider the limitations of a pension in terms of a mortgage. A personal pension cannot be cashed in before you are fifty, so you could find it impossible to pay off the mortgage earlier than planned if your fund performs better than expected. Pension benefits, quite logically, can only be taken at retirement, and for personal pensions you can choose that to be any time between the ages of fifty and seventy-five. Remember, you don't have to retire to take your pension, and the fund can also be taken in segments. A good adviser will be able to help you sidestep this problem should it occur. You may need to persuade the lender to increase the term of your pension mortgage to a later retirement.

Finally, there is the possible effect of future legislation. This is always a risk with personal finance products that are used to achieve something they were not originally designed for. The government's tacit disapproval of pension mortgages could result in legal changes to make them more difficult to use. There is also a risk that the government will change the rules about the final lump sum: if it decides to tax it, or even abolish it altogether, you could have problems paying back the money you owe on your property.

Historically, where governments have tightened up tax legislation, they have rarely, if ever, made new laws retroactive. If you already have a pension mortgage, the contract details are therefore unlikely to be affected by future tax changes. The only major risk would arise if you were to stop paying the premium for a time. This could happen in a period of unemployment, for example. If tax changes are introduced while the pension is frozen, you may find yourself subject to a new and less beneficial regime when you start paying premiums again. This problem can be avoided by ensuring that your pension plan is flexible enough to be restarted if you need to take a contributions 'holiday'. One last warning: some contributions holidays may be limited to one year before the company makes the plan 'paid up'. Make sure your plan comes with indefinite premium holiday entitlements.

Foreign currency mortgages

Foreign currency mortgages are the same as any other mortgage except that the advance is made in a currency other than sterling. When interest rates in the UK are high, such a mortgage can appear very attractive. At any given time, another country is bound to have lower interest rates than the UK.

Unfortunately, because of possible currency movements, mortgages in a foreign currency are extremely risky. The danger, as anyone running an export business will tell you, is in having assets and liabilities in different currencies. You might, for example, have the debt (the mortgage advance) in Swiss francs, while your assets (your income and the value of the property) remain in sterling. Any movement between the two currencies will have an immediate effect on your financial strength. If you borrowed £100,000 worth of Swiss francs and the value of sterling fell by 10 per cent against the Swiss franc, your debt would instantly become £110,000. Of course, the reverse is also true: if the value of sterling appreciated against the other currency, your mortgage debt would decrease.

One or two companies have promised a service which would closely monitor currency movements and move your debt into another currency if the one you are in starts looking too strong. If they do their job properly, the benefits can be enormous. Theoretically, your debt could be wiped out simply by speculation! But even the most successful foreign currency dealers will warn you that mortgages of this kind are suitable only if you can afford to lose large sums of money. For someone labouring under burdensome interest rates and already finding it hard to make ends meet, they are neither a safe nor a cheap alternative.

My own view is that these are difficult to manage and extremely risky. Although I have seen examples of people doing well out of them, many more have lost money.

Lifetime mortgages

Lifetime mortgages have so far failed to take off in the UK. Unlike a lot of financial wizardry, this is a home-grown concept, which several companies claim to have pioneered. Under current market conditions they are unlikely to find many takers, but they could be worth looking at if property values begin to rise steadily again.

The concept is based on the type of interest-only loan you would normally have as part of an endowment, PEP, unit trust, investment trust, or pension mortgage. The lender gives you an advance and your monthly repayments consist entirely of interest. The capital will be paid back at some later stage when whichever investment you choose has grown by the required amount. The difference with a lifetime mortgage is that the lender does not want to know how you intend to pay the money back. Its only concerns are that you earn enough money to meet the interest payments and that the property is worth more than the amount you borrow. Nor does it insist that you pay back the loan by a specific date. In fact, provided you carry on making the interest payments, the lender will be happy if you never pay it back. When you die the debt will be recouped from the sale of the property.

Looking back at how the property market performed at the end of the 1980s through to the beginning of the 1990s, this may seem complete madness. Yet, for both borrower and lender, lifetime mortgages are extremely useful. Their efficiency depends entirely on a steady inflationary increase in house prices and prices generally.

As an example, imagine that the annual inflation rate for both property and prices will average 5 per cent over the next 25 years. Today you take out a £50,000 lifetime mortgage on a property currently worth £60,000. In 25 years the debt will have reduced to less than £14,000 at today's prices, while the value of the property will have risen to over £200,000. Your mortgage debt will have reduced to less than 7 per cent of the property value. In other words, the proportion of the property you own will have risen from 17 per cent to 93 per cent purely as a result of inflation. The loan repayments will, likewise, have become easier: monthly repayments of £300 will have dwindled to just over £20 at today's prices. Even if you will be retired or living in otherwise reduced financial circumstances, you will be more likely to be able to continue servicing the debt even if you do not have the capital to clear it completely.

The few lenders offering this type of loan hope borrowers use it as the basis of their lifelong financial planning. If they need money, they can raise a loan against the equity of their property and pay it back when they are able to. The debt can also be transferred from one property to another so that, as the value increases, the borrower can move up the property ladder. On paper it looks an excellent plan. In the early stages of its development some lenders even toyed with the idea of giving borrowers chequebooks and paying-in books so they could gain access to the equity tied up in their property as easily as they could the money in their bank accounts. The only limitation on how much they could 'draw out' would be their ability to service the debt and the market value of their property.

For gay men such mortgages are ideal provided the lender does not insist on a whole-of-life assurance contract to cover the loan in case you die. Having secured the loan, you will have dispensed with any problems in obtaining a mortgage or moving up the property ladder. The availability of lifetime mortgages is still very limited. But for the property slump, they would probably be much better known by now. However, in spite of the problems many mortgage lenders are still facing, it may be possible to find one prepared to lend money on this basis.

LOANS v. INTEREST RATES

Within these broad types of loan there are various ways in which the lender can structure the regular interest payments. The most common method is a basic variable-rate mortgage. After you have borrowed the money, interest will be charged at regular intervals at a rate determined by the underlying base rate (the interest rate the main UK commercial banks charge for loans). If the base rate increases or decreases, so too does the level of your loan repayments. This caused problems for borrowers towards the end of the 1980s, when the government increased interest rates in a bid to reduce consumer spending and halt inflation. Demand was growing too quickly and threatened to damage the government's low inflation policy. In a short space of time, interest rates doubled and so too did the cost of variable-interest mortgages. For many it was just too much, and the UK debt burden increased to a level from which it is still trying to recover.

Fixed-interest loans

An alternative is a fixed-interest loan. With these you agree a set rate of interest with the lender at the outset. No matter what happens to the underlying base rate, you will continue paying the same amount. In some ways this makes it something of a gamble: if you lock yourself into a fixed rate and the base rate falls, you will be worse off than if you had chosen a variable-rate mortgage. Even so, it does protect you against a possible interest rate hike in the short term, and allows you to budget carefully during the early days of your mortgage.

In most cases the period for which the interest is fixed is only the initial period of the loan – usually from one to three years. Sometimes further fixed-interest periods are available, but at different rates. Unfortunately, fixed-interest loans are more frequently available when interest rates are falling. When they look set to rise over a long period of time, lenders are understandably reluctant to offer them. But in some financial climates the view of the money markets is that interest rates will rise in the short term but fall in the long term. Cash may then be found at low fixed rates, in spite of threatened interest rate increases.

A variation on this theme is the 'cap-and-collar' loan. This is a halfway house between fixed-rate and variable-rate mortgages. When the loan is arranged the lender promises that, although the rate of interest may fluctuate, it will stay within a fixed band.

Low-start schemes

When mortgages look expensive, either because of booming property prices or high interest rates, lenders come up with numerous schemes for making house purchase more affordable. But be cautious of these: it is rare for a lender to offer you something for nothing. Some schemes fall into the 'low-start' category. When you begin the mortgage you are charged a lower interest rate than those with a standard variable-rate loan. Repayments continue for a while in this way but gradually grow until, after a few years, you find yourself paying more interest than those on a standard variable rate. The lender makes no apologies for this. The theory is that during the initial stages, when a mortgage is relatively very expensive, you need as much help as possible. After a few years inflation will have eroded the real value of your payments and, to boot, you will probably be on a much higher salary. In practice it can still be a painful experience when you begin paying the full amount. If you are going to consider a low-start scheme, you must be realistic about whether you will be able to afford the repayments when the interest rate goes up.

With the most painful type of deferred loan, the difference between what you pay and the actual variable interest rate accumulates and is added to your original advance in the form of a debt. Not only do you pay an inflated rate of interest on the loan in later years, but it is applied to a bigger loan than you started with.

PROPERTY INSURANCE

No matter which type of mortgage you choose, it is essential to arrange property insurance. With this type of cover, sexuality should never be a factor. The only exception is if an insurance company is marketing some kind of package deal which, as well as property insurance, contains elements of health and sickness or life cover. Lenders will usually insist the property be insured with a reputable company before the advance is made. In some cases the lender will handle the insurance and ask you to send a cheque covering the premium before forwarding the policy to you. Under the terms of the Fair Trading Act, a lender is unable to prevent you from shopping around for insurance if you feel the policy it wants to sell you is too expensive; in practice, lenders make it difficult. Even if you find a highly competitive company that the lender agrees is a reputable one, it will probably demand a payment from you if you choose *not* to be insured by one of the panel of companies it uses. This so-called administration charge will almost certainly be enough to destroy the competitive edge the cheaper company may have.

Things are slightly different if you are offered a loan carrying a special discount. With these mortgages the lender can make all sorts of demands about what sort of policy you should have, even insisting you buy a contents policy (see p. 73) from them. As usual, companies are very good at honouring the letter of the law rather than the spirit.

Property insurance will cover most major risks like fire, flood, or accidents. It will often also cover the building against subsidence, but this may be excluded if your property is in an area which already has a history of subsidence. In recent years insurance companies have been heavily hit by subsidence claims following alternating extremes of heavy rain and long dry periods in the UK. The chances are that an insurance company will be more wary of insuring against subsidence, so make sure you are covered.

Regional variations

The increasingly regionalized claims experience of property insurers has caused another change. A few years ago most companies levied the same premium charge per £1000 worth of property value no matter where you lived. Now some areas are likely to be more expensive than others. In parts of the country where individual companies have suffered particularly badly, they may be trying to offload the risk completely, sometimes by making their premiums uncompetitive. For this reason, especially if you are given a frighteningly high quotation or are offered a policy with a long list of exclusions, shop around and see if any other companies can give you a better deal. Once again, an independent adviser should be able to help.

How much cover?

In assessing the level of cover you need, you should take into account how the property market is doing. Policies are generally renewed annually. When property values are moving rapidly upwards, it is better to insure for the amount you estimate the property will be worth in a year's time rather than what it is worth now. If the property is completely destroyed no insurance company will be persuaded to pay out more than the maximum sum insured that you have paid for, even if your property turns out to be more expensive to replace than you thought. A quick look at the price of similar properties in your local estate agent's window will give you an idea of the value. If the big lenders, like the Halifax, claim property values are moving up by, say, 10 per cent annually, add that percentage to the current value of your property. That way, if you have to make a claim eleven months after you take out the policy, you will not find yourself thousands of pounds out of pocket.

The same is true with smaller claims. Just because your home is insured for a maximum of £100,000, it does not necessarily follow that the insurance company will pay out £20,000 for damage caused by a fire in the kitchen. If the company's loss adjuster thinks you have skimped on the premium and are 20 per cent underinsured, he may deduct the same percentage from your final settlement.

If, on the other hand, the market is falling, there is little point in insuring for more than the property's current value. Some insurance companies attempt to push up maximum sums assured (and therefore the premiums they charge) by saying that it always costs more to rebuild a house than to buy it in the first place. Salesmen happily claim that once you have added solicitor's and surveyor's fees, the cost of demolishing what's left of the old building, and the cost of renting alternative accommodation while yours is being rebuilt, your costs will have exceeded the house's current market value. They say it is prudent, therefore, to add a percentage to the property's market value. In terms of premiums, this 'percentage' could add quite a bit to your insurance costs. Whether or not it is necessary is arguable, for it depends on a number of factors. Most of all, it depends on how high property prices are and the costs of materials and labour. In addition, it is all very well over-insuring, but you should make sure your insurance includes all the things your insurance man claims will push up the replacement cost of your property. Will your insurance company simply hand over a cheque and let you get on with it, or will it want to monitor the whole process itself? If it handles everything itself, is it prepared to rebuild the house you lost? Will it rehouse you while the work is going on or do you have to find the money for that yourself? Any doubts about the rebuilding costs of your property can usually be cleared up by referring to the structural survey (if you had one carried out), which may well give an estimated cost. If not, ask a surveyor.

Another thing to consider when looking at overall property values is the cost of the land. Unlike buildings, land is rarely destroyed unless it collapses into a hole or, with coastal property, slides into the sea like a Scarborough hotel. With the probability of the land remaining, it should be remembered that this is a major part of your property's overall value.

If you make any structural changes to the property between renewal periods, make sure you update the amount of cover. Where you are insured via the lender, this can usually be a matter of picking up the phone and letting the people at your local branch know. You will be covered for the extra amount immediately, and billed for the extra premium on the renewal date. Your lender will probably also keep you covered if you fail to pay the premium, simply by adding the premium cost to the total capital outstanding until you pay it. So if you decide to use a cheaper or otherwise more competitive insurance company, let your lender know in advance and in writing, otherwise you could end up with two insurance policies. If you have a claim, you will still only be covered by one.

CONTENTS INSURANCE

Contents insurance, as the name suggests, covers your furniture and other household items. Some insurance companies offer combined buildings and contents cover in one policy. (Be aware, though, that a company offering good terms for one type of cover is not necessarily the best for both.) But it is usually a separate type of cover, and it works in a different way. Broadly, there are two types of contents insurance: standard cover, and new-for-old.

Standard cover is cheaper, but can be ineffective if the contents of your home are getting on a bit. This is because insurance policies often operate under the principle of indemnification: that someone who makes a claim should be restored to the position they were in before the claim was made. While this means you will not be any worse off, it also prevents you from being better off. A claim for a dining room suite which is twenty years old under a standard policy will pay out only the adjudged second-hand value of the equivalent suite. New-for-old policies are more expensive but, under the same claim, the replacement furniture would be brand new.

Gay partners living together should make sure that both their names appear on the policy document, so that all their house contents are covered and not just those belonging to one of them.

There are often misunderstandings about exactly what contents insurance covers. People complain that they have been duped by the small print of a policy when, in fact, careful reading of the contract before they signed it would have made things quite clear. Contents policies nearly always cover you against fire, flood, and theft, but under each of these headings there can be grey areas. A hole burned in a shirt while you are ironing can be claimed as fire damage with some companies, but others will say there was no fire unless there was ignition – everything else is 'scorching'.

The commonest error people make is that their policy covers them against accidental damage. Most policies do not, but there are companies offering such cover. Its inclusion sends premiums sky-high. Once again, though, it is worth shopping around. A few policies on the market offer limited accidental damage clauses as part of their standard contracts and, apparently, at no extra charge. Electrical goods are one example. Some insurers will replace your TV, video, or hi-fi no matter how they are damaged: if you knock over the video while cleaning or put your foot through the TV screen, you will be able to claim. This is important cover if you are renting equipment. The rental company will often need to be reassured that their equipment is covered while it is in your house. Other companies may be prepared to cover certain precious items against accidental breakage.

All risks

Although some contents insurance includes temporary cover for items while they are removed from the home, it is best to buy an all-risks policy for jewellery or other valuables you often carry with you. If they are lost, damaged, or stolen the insurance company will cover the cost. For relatively inexpensive items it may not be necessary to declare each one individually. The insurer will usually offer you a certain amount of cover for an unspecified number of items. Within this maximum a set percentage can be claimed for any one item. For extremely valuable objects, the insurance company may insist that each one is valued by an independent assessor.

Another classic misconception about contents insurance is that it covers against wear and tear. I have yet to find a policy that does. Furniture gets old and pictures fade. Insurance is about risk, not certainty.

Regional variations

Contents insurance, more so than buildings insurance, shows wide regional variations. The main reason for this is the effect of crime statistics in particular areas. Metropolitan centres like London, Birmingham, and Liverpool have suffered enormous hikes in premiums for contents insurance during the last few years. In some cases insurance companies are quite willing to admit they are uninterested in insuring people in those areas. As with most insurance cover, this places those who need it most in the anomalous position of not being able to get it – unless they are prepared to pay through the nose. Many simply go without. There seems to be hardly any way out of this dilemma, unless you can find a company which offers insurance cover just against the relatively low-risk fire and flood, not theft. Some companies may be prepared to issue cover for theft in high-risk areas if you can demonstrate that you have made your home more secure, perhaps by fitting a burglar alarm, mortice deadlock, and window bolts. It may be cheaper to buy yourself a huge alsatian dog.

What mortgage?

In spite of the numerous types of mortgage available, choosing one is straightforward enough. The broad choice you have to make is between a repayment loan – where a portion of the capital is paid back with each repayment – or an interest-only loan backed by an endowment, PEP, pension, unit trust, investment trust, or nothing at all. Figures from the Building Societies Association show endowment mortgages to be the overwhelming favourite, accounting for 70 per cent of all UK home loans.

Much depends on what you want to achieve with your mortgage. If, like most people, you just want something that will pay back your loan, is flexible enough to cope with future house purchases, and which may also deliver a cash sum at the end of the term, take the endowment route. If you are happy to take on a little extra risk for the sake of perhaps paying off your mortgage early or receiving a larger (or smaller) cash sum at the end of the mortgage term, take one of the equity-based options.

Other decisions about whether to take a deferred interest scheme or a fixed-rate loan will depend pretty much on your financial position. The thing to be wary of, though, is that apparently cut-price mortgages usually have a sting in the tail. While they may be affordable in the early stages they tend to become more expensive than standard variable-rate loans in later years. If you are not confident that your income will improve during the next few years, it's best to avoid such low-start deals.

Financially, for many homeowners their house is more than their home – it is the biggest investment they will ever make. It is to ways of investing your spare cash that we turn in the next chapter.

4

INVESTMENT

We all understand that saving and investment broadly means putting money aside for use at some later date. But the huge variety of ways this can be done makes it a potentially bewildering area of personal finance. Anything from stuffing money under the mattress to moving capital around the world stock markets comes under this heading. Even working out what are savings and what are investments can be tricky, and the two definitions are often interchangeable. But generally, investment is the name given to more speculative ways of putting money aside. Investors take calculated risks with their money in the hope of making it grow; if things go wrong, they may lose some or all of it. Savers usually prefer not to risk their money. They need to be assured that whatever they put aside will be kept safe until they need it, and if they can watch it grow at the same time then so much the better.

Yet few of us fall strictly into one category or the other. Successful financial planning, for most people, is based on a mix of different types of saving and investment offering various levels of risk and reward. There are bound to be people at both ends of the scale who are either over-cautious or totally reckless, but neither is likely to find their money working for them as effectively as it could.

Exactly how you should plan your finances depends on your particular circumstances. For gay men, the various types of investment assume a different degree of importance than for heterosexuals. The biggest obstacle gay men face when planning their finances is in buying life cover. Although for many gay men these problems can be over-come, there are some who will find themselves uninsurable. Those already diagnosed HIV positive are most likely to be excluded. There are many other gay men who simply refuse to put themselves through the mill in the way insurance companies demand.

If you are one of these people, you must find ways of organizing your finances so as to sidestep the need for life assurance. Whether looking for a way of paying off a mortgage, funding your retirement, or providing for dependants after you die, savings and investments can often help. You may already have some idea of how you would like to make your money work for you; if not, or if your personal circumstances are complicated, you may prefer talking to a professional financial adviser. Much depends on how long you want to tie your money up for, the amount of risk you are prepared to take, and the level of return you expect.

Deposit accounts

The most basic form of saving, apart from the jar on the mantelpiece, is an interest-bearing deposit account with either a bank or a building society. These offer three main benefits. First, your money is safe – managers of deposit accounts are unlikely to dash down to the nearest casino and put your life savings on 23 red. Money on deposit is used mainly to fund loans made by banks and building societies. In many cases, as with mortgages, these will be secured against assets. Second, your money will grow. A portion of the interest banks and building societies charge borrowers is passed on to depositors. Third, you can normally get at your money whenever you need to.

Each bank or building society offers a range of deposit accounts offering different interest rates. The larger the amount you save and the longer you save it for, the better the interest rate. Most accounts have investment bands at, say, £5000, £10,000, and so on. As your savings build up and pass each of these levels, the rate of interest increases. Access to your account can also vary. The top-paying accounts usually restrict you to 90-day access: if you want to make a withdrawal, you have to let the bank or building society manager know at least 90 days in advance. This is not to say that you will be prevented from drawing out cash if you need to. Rather, if you fail to give the required notice of withdrawal, you simply lose a proportion of the interest you would otherwise have earned.

Many high-interest accounts are now offering the type of benefits usually associated with current accounts. Many supply chequebooks, and a growing number provide cheque guarantee cards. The main drawback with deposit accounts is that the level of return they offer is very limited. When interest rates are high, as they were during the early 1990s, the return on investments can be quite respectable. At other times, especially when the economy is growing strongly, investors should look elsewhere for capital growth. This does not mean that deposit accounts should not form part of your financial plan. Generally, investors find deposit accounts a little too unexciting. Unless you need to have cash available quickly or you want to consolidate financial gains made in a more volatile investment, they can be unappealing.

Cash unit trusts

For people who require the security of a deposit account but would prefer high interest and instant access, there is a far better alternative to standard building society accounts. It should be remembered that building societies and banks must cover the expense of sometimes very large branch networks. This huge overhead reduces the amount of cash that can be paid out as interest. Unit trust companies are not burdened in the same way and some, like Fidelity Investments and Gartmore Fund Managers, offer cash funds. These can be bought directly from the unit trust company or through a financial adviser. Some cash funds also offer benefits typical of a high street bank, like cheque-books and cheque guarantee cards. Very often, too, they do not have the 'front-end' charges typical of other types of unit trust. Interest averages 2 per cent more than is offered by building societies or banks with their 90-day accounts.

Stocks and shares

Although people often associate investment in stocks and shares with big businessmen, City whiz-kids, and wealthy speculators, most of those who invest on the stock market are of the slow and steady kind. Stocks and shares, often described generically as equities, represent investment in private or public enterprises, and are traded between buyers and sellers. The distinction between them is not clear cut, but in the UK stocks are generally fixed-interest investments such as government securities, while shares give the investor part-ownership of a 'listed' company – one whose shares are traded on the London Stock Exchange. If there are 100,000 of a company's shares on the market and you buy 50,000 of them, you own half the company. At this proportion of ownership shareholders usually have some say over how the company operates and will probably have members on its board to represent their interests. Most shareholders have much smaller holdings, and are interested only in the value of the shares they hold. This value is determined purely by the level of demand for a particular share. If it is very popular, the value rises; if there are more sellers than buyers, the value drops – just like any commodity.

Shares usually also offer returns in the form of dividends. Dividends represent a portion of the company's profits, paid out to its shareholders each year. How high these are depends on how well the company is faring. In bad years there may be little or no profit at all. Investors (or their financial advisers) looking for income from shares will try to pick those with the best dividend prospects.

The level of demand for stocks and shares – and therefore their value – is mainly affected by the fortunes of the company the shares represent. If profits are rising, for example, the company's shares will be more sought after than if it were in financial trouble. But even apparently healthy companies can have problems. The departure of a key board member can make investors nervous about the company's future and cause them to start selling shares. A company heavily dependent on exports could see its share price fall if currency movements make it less competitive abroad. Even an offhand comment can lead to mass selling of shares.

Knowing when to buy and when to sell is the basic key to stock market success. Unfortunately, as with most things, it isn't that easy. The prices of shares traded on the London Stock Exchange are published daily in the *Financial Times* and other newspapers. Share prices are listed under a number of 'sectors': banks, brewers and distillers, business services, and so on. The overall performance of the stock market is represented by indices such as the FTSE 100 Index or the FT-Actuaries All-Share Index. The FTSE 100 (called 'Footsie') plots the changing value of the top 100 shares traded on the London Stock Exchange. It started in 1983 at a base of 1000, and has since (by December 1993) risen to over 3000.

The FT-Actuaries All-Share Index plots the progress of all shares listed in London. The larger index gives a more representative figure, but the smaller one is easier to calculate. The difficulty in picking the right shares is demonstrated by the performance of professional investment managers, 'fund managers', relative to the stock market indices. Professional managers are employed by investment companies to look after their clients' money. When you invest in pensions, unit trusts, or insurance policies it is the investment manager who makes the daily decisions about which investment your money goes into.

A thoroughly skilful investor would buy a share when it was cheapest (when its value had fallen as far as it could go) and sell at the top of the market (when its value had risen as far as it could and was about to fall again). An investor who could do this would perform better than the indices. In fact, more than half of all UK investment managers fare a good deal worse than the index – whichever one they choose. There are plenty of theories floating around about how to beat the market, in much the same way as people claim to have guaranteed systems for roulette or horse racing. The truth is that it takes a lot of effort to stay on top of investment in stocks and shares. There is much to be said for making a broad range of investments in companies from different stock market sectors, and simply letting them look after themselves. Even with the ups and downs of the late 1980s, funds invested in this way, known as tracker funds, did better than deposit accounts over a five-year period.

Tracker funds are based on a particular index – the FTSE 100, for example – and are managed according to a mathematical formula. The manager buys the shares of all the companies in the index in varying proportions according to how many shares each company has in the stock market. A fund built in this way should perform in pretty much the same way as the index itself. Trackers are favoured by those who are confident that the index will perform well over long periods, in spite of occasional setbacks. There is no guarantee that this will happen, but managers are often keen to point out that in the past stock markets have outperformed many other forms of investment over the long term. Pension fund managers, in particular, frequently put their faith in tracker funds and often include at least one as part of clients' portfolios. Some unit trust managers offer them to private investors too, although there are not a great number on the market at the moment.

But even if you closely follow company news and keep an eye out for anything that could affect share prices, you could still be caught out. In the crash of October 1987, some of the country's most renowned investment managers were left holding shares that had been stripped of their value.

Nobody without a great deal of spare time and money they can afford to lose should even dream of trying to turn a fast buck on the stock market. But this does not mean that everyone else should not invest in equities. Statistics show that, over the longer term, stocks and shares deliver better returns than most other forms of investment. One of the great tragedies of the 1987 crash was that many new investors – mainly those who had benefited from the government's privatization programme – panicked and sold their shares, never to return to the stock market. If, instead, they had bought even more shares while they were cheap, and hung on to them, they would have been a lot better off today. For those with neither the time nor vast sums of money to blow on the stock market there are still a number of ways of taking advantage of the possible gains.

Portfolio management

Most stockbrokers offer managed portfolio services. Once you have worked out how much money you want to invest, the stockbroker will help you put together a portfolio of shares according to what type of investment performance you want. If, for example, you want your initial investment to be secure, providing income and a degree of capital growth, the stockbroker will be able to advise how best to do it. On the other hand, if you want something racier, your stockbroker can arrange for that too.

Portfolio services usually divide into two types: discretionary and advisory. With a discretionary service, the portfolio is managed by the stockbroker without reference to his client. Once client and stockbroker have agreed an investment strategy, it is down to the stockbroker to decide what to buy or sell and when. The client will be kept fully informed about what is happening, but only after the event. An advisory service is different: the stockbroker consults with the client before doing anything. Although this will usually take the form of a strong recommendation from the stockbroker, the final decision rests with the client.

Charges for this type of service vary greatly, and choosing a stockbroker can be harder than choosing equities yourself. Some will charge a commission on all transactions. Often this is 1.65 per cent – a figure which used to be the standard commission charge before the City was reformed several years ago. Very often, even when a percentage is quoted, there is a minimum charge per transaction, typically £15 to £50. Some stockbrokers simply charge a flat fee for the work they do, often according to the portfolio you put together. The minimum level of investment demanded by stockbrokers gives an indication of the type of net worth you need to benefit fully from their service. Some will insist you have £300,000 plus before they even look at you. But plenty of stockbrokers will look at much smaller sums, and a few ask for no minimum investment at all.

But although £10,000, say, might seem a lot of cash to an individual investor, it will not buy a huge number of shares. By the time the stockbroker's fees have been deducted, the investment will be even less effective. Knowing at what level of investment to employ a stockbroker is difficult. The thing to remember is that bigger sums can be more easily invested: with a large amount of cash, a stockbroker will be able to spread the risk on your portfolio by investing in a wide spread of equities. Charges will also have a less damaging effect with larger sums.

This does not mean those with £10,000 to invest should avoid equity investment completely. A growing number of small investors are now making use of dealing-only services, such as Sharelink, which carry out the buy and sell orders of clients at competitive costs. Other discount stockbrokers who cut costs by transacting no-frills share deals (they do not advise you on what to buy and sell) include Fidelity Brokers and, a newcomer to the UK market, Charles Schwab from the USA. But there are other ways for smaller investors to gain exposure to the stock market.

Unit trusts

These are the most common type of pooled equity invest-ment in the UK. Instead of buying individual stocks and shares, investors buy units from a fund manager. The manager pools cash from hundreds of investors and uses it to build a portfolio of stocks and shares. The cost of units in the trust depends on how well the underlying investments are performing. If they are doing well, the unit price will increase; if the value of the underlying investments is falling, the value of the units will fall as well.

There are many different types of unit trust on the market offering different investment profiles. Most unit trust managers offer a range of different types. Very often, by investing in one of the manager's savings plans, investors can switch between different unit trusts as their investment needs change.

As with stocks and shares, unit trusts fall into various categories. In particular, there are unit trusts that buy shares from particular countries or regions. So if you think that investment prospects in Europe or the Far East look good, you choose from several unit trusts covering those areas. There are also unit trusts specializing in certain sectors, such as gold funds, which concentrate on the shares of gold-mining companies. For those who prefer not to be so specific, there are general funds investing in a very broad range of shares. Within each sector there are unit trusts offering a choice of either accumulation units aimed at building your capital investment, or income units where the dividends on shares the unit trust manager invests in are distributed to the investors rather than reinvested in the fund.

In recent years the number of ethical funds on the market has mushroomed. These avoid investing in areas that some people object to. Common exclusions include South Africa (though this may be changing as the country moves towards majority rule), the arms industry, and the fur trade. Most ethical funds will also have a bias towards companies or countries making positive efforts in certain areas. There are now a number of 'green' funds on the market investing in environmentally friendly areas.

The variety of unit trusts on the market can make choosing one seem as complex as picking individual stocks and shares. The main question to ask yourself before investing in any pooled investment is how good the manager is at delivering the goods. The performance of unit trusts is very easy to check. Unit prices are published every day in the *Financial Times* under the heading 'Managed Funds'. Funds are grouped by manager rather than by sector, so you can see the range of unit trusts offered by each manager and how they are performing. If you are already invested in a unit trust you can use the *FT* to see how much your investment is currently worth. Although it can be tricky for investors with no experience of the investment market to check out a fund manager, this is something an independent financial adviser can help with.

Smaller funds are often more volatile than larger ones because the money available to be invested in them buys fewer shares. A sharp movement in a particular share price may, therefore, have a more dramatic effect on a small

fund's value than on a fund investing in the shares of more
companies. Such volatility can be both good and bad.
Although there is a risk of the value falling faster than in
a bigger fund, it may rise faster too. Remember, though,
that what might start out as a small, high-performing fund
could become larger and less prone to bigger peaks and
troughs as more investors are attracted to it. Its former high
performance could then become a thing of the past.

Apart from checking out both the manager and its unit
trusts before making a choice, you should also compare
charges. There are most commonly two main charges to
watch for with unit trusts: the initial charge and the annual
management charge. The initial charge is normally paid up
front, and covers the administration costs of setting up the
scheme – usually it represents around 5 per cent of your
investment. If you bought into the unit trust via a financial
adviser, this will normally include his commission. Some
advisers, especially those who charge fees, will often waive
all or part of their commission, which can cut the initial
charge by up to two-thirds. The initial charge is rarely
reduced by buying units directly from the manager rather
than through a financial adviser. Companies offering this
sort of discount may be poor managers desperate for new
business.

A good adviser with a broad understanding of the investment market can be well worth paying commission to.
Unless you are sure of what unit trust to buy, it is best to
take professional independent advice. The annual management charge is much smaller, usually around 0.75 per cent.
This covers the on-going management of the fund. Some
fund managers sneak in additional charges, and it is as well
to make sure you are clear about exactly how much is
deducted each year from your investment. A particular unit

trust might seem attractive if it has put on 25 per cent capital growth, but this will be of little use if most of such gains are swallowed up in charges.

Bid/offer spread is the most common front-end charge and represents the difference between the amount for which the unit manager will sell units to an investor (the offer price) and how much he will pay to buy them back (the bid price). The gap between these two prices is usually 5 per cent.

Two particular charges to watch out for are capital units and nil-allocation units. Capital units cost more than other units, and the difference between their cost and the real unit cost is creamed off by the fund manager. Capital units are usually charged for a specific period when an investor first puts money into a unit trust. With nil-allocation units, the manager takes all the money you pay in to cover his charges. In the early days of a unit trust savings plan making these charges, none of the money you pay goes towards buying units which you can sell later. Aside from these possible pitfalls unit trusts are generally very open about their charges, making it very easy to see what you get for your money.

As with most types of pooled investment, unit trusts take both lump-sum and regular payments. While some investors will have a one-off sum of money they want to invest, others like to pay regular amounts into a plan and watch their money grow. Some, especially those working for themselves, combine both investment methods. They commit a specific amount to be paid into a unit trust at regular intervals. Then, if they find they have a bit more cash available later, they can invest that too.

Although there isn't much to choose between regular and lump-sum investments, there is one particular advantage that regular schemes have. When stock markets are volatile, the price of units in unit trusts can fluctuate wildly up and down. All you can hope for in these circumstances is that in spite of the troughs the overall trend is upwards. If you bought all your units in one go, the value of your investment will rise and fall with the market. But those who pay a set premium each month will be less susceptible to volatility. This is because of a principle called pound cost averaging. If, for example, you pay £100 each month into a unit trust and the cost per unit is £1, you buy 100 units each time. When you sell them back to the manager in a few years' time, you hope the value is much higher. In a volatile market the unit price may drop – but then your £100 goes a lot further. At 50p a unit you would get twice as many units for your £100. When unit prices are cheap you get more of them for your money, so in particular months you may buy more units than in other months. And when the value picks up again, as you hope it will, you will have considerably more units to sell than if the unit price had not fallen in the meantime.

Some advisers may suggest that the lower charges on single premium payments into unit trust savings make them more cost effective than regular payments. The thing to bear in mind here is where such money will be saved in the interim. Simply putting it on deposit in lieu of regular payments into a unit trust until you have enough to make a single payment will exclude your savings from any stock market gains for as long as it takes you to save the necessary cash. You will not suffer from any market slumps either, but having made the decision to opt for unit trust or unit linked savings you have presumably already weighed up the risk and chosen to take it. In that case you will probably want your savings to gain as much exposure to the stock market as possible. Holding back for the sake of lower charges could be a false economy.

Unit trust portfolio services

Unit trusts form the basis for many other investment products. Some unit trust managers even offer portfolio services similar to those offered by stockbrokers for equity investors. The big difference with this scaled-down version of an equity portfolio is that by using unit trusts rather than direct investment in stocks and shares, much smaller sums can be invested effectively. The majority of unit trust portfolio services have a minimum investment of £10,000; a few have no minimum at all, while others start as low as £1000 or £2000. As with equity portfolio services, unit trust portfolios may be discretionary or advisory.

The advantage that unit trust portfolio management services have over other types of managed fund is that the portfolio can be geared to the individual investment needs of the investor. While some managers, like stockbrokers, will sit down with a client and work out a strategy, most have a range of portfolios offering various investment objectives. Some are geared to providing a monthly income, while others concentrate on high capital growth or a combination of capital growth and income. There are portfolios that focus on certain types of investment: overseas equity, gilts and fixed interest stock, or currency.

The popularity of unit trust portfolios is one area of investment marred by the arrival of the Financial Services Act in 1986. To get the most out of a portfolio, the manager needs to be able to access as many unit trusts as possible. In the UK there are well over 1500 individual unit trusts. Before the Act became law managers could offer clients a choice of any UK unit trust. (To what extent they actually did this rather than recommend their own funds is another matter.) Now, anyone offering investment advice must declare themselves to be either tied (they represent the interests of a particular investment company) or independent (they will recommend the product most suitable to your financial needs, no matter which company sells it). Managers offering unit trust portfolio services also sell unit trusts. If they claimed to be offering independent advice, there might be an apparent conflict of interest if they recommended that a client invest in their own unit trust. Some unit trust managers withdrew the service altogether, while others found ways round it: offering the service via a sister company, for example, or on an execution-only basis (this means they would not promote their product, but if a client approached the manager first he could still legally invest in it). More often, managers simply began recommending their own unit trusts. This is fine and dandy if the manager's own unit trusts perform well, but if they do not you could incur heavy charges simply for the privilege of having your cash moved from one second-rate unit trust to another.

As with equity portfolio services, charges vary. Some services will levy an annual charge representing a percentage of the value of your portfolio, typically between 0.5 and 1 per cent. Others charge an annual fee, often between £250 and £500. Working out which method is the most cost effective depends on how much money you have invested. There are also a number of unit trust products on the market offering the same benefits as a unit trust portfolio service where the client can only access one manager's funds. These are frequently cheaper than unit trust portfolios, but just as effective. Under one product heading the client can gain access to a range of the company's unit trusts. The initial and annual charges will often also include a number of free switches between funds.

Insurance company bonds

Insurance company bonds, usually known as 'investment bonds', are much the same as unit trusts, other than occasionally offering a wider range of funds and a little more flexibility. In fact, many bonds are invested in unit trust funds. The main difference is in the tax paid on them.

Unit trusts are subject to CGT, so any gains over the CGT threshold (currently £5800) in the tax year of encashment will be taxed at your personal tax rate. Exceptionally large encashments in any one year may result in a very large tax bill, expecially if you pay tax at the highest rate. Investors prepared to make small annual encashments may find this tax treatment very effective, however. Dividends from a unit trust are paid net of basic-rate tax, which non-taxpayers can reclaim from the Inland Revenue.

Bonds are not subject to basic-rate income tax. Provided the gain in any one tax year does not push you into a higher-rate tax bracket, it will be tax-free. If you encash a bond as a higher-rate taxpayer, or if the gain pushes you into a higher tax bracket, you will be subject to the higher-rate 'slice' of tax. At present this is 15 per cent, the difference between the 25 per cent basic rate and the 40 per cent higher rate. Over a 20-year period, bonds allow you to strip out the initial investment at a rate of 5 per cent for every year you have owned them, without any tax liability whatsoever. This means that even higher-rate taxpayers can enjoy a tax-free income of 5 per cent a year.

Investment trusts

Investment trusts are in some ways similar to unit trusts. There are, however, important differences. Investment trusts are possibly the oldest form of pooled investment. As with unit trusts, investors make regular or lump-sum savings which are then managed on their behalf by the investment trust manager. The main difference between the two types of trust is in their basic structure. A unit trust expands to accommodate new investment. When a new investor joins it, new units are created, and when someone sells their units, they are usually cancelled (or sometimes simply passed on to a new investor). When there are more buyers than sellers the unit trust becomes bigger; when there are more sellers than buyers the unit trust shrinks. The value of each unit is simply the asset value of the trust divided by the number of units.

Investment trusts are actually companies. Instead of buying units, you buy shares in them. The number of shares in issue remains the same unless, like any typical company, the investment trust decides to issue more. As with any typical shares the value of investment trust shares depends entirely on demand. If there are plenty of buyers the price goes up; if there are few the price drops. This means that the total value of an investment trust's shares may be different to the value of its underlying assets. If the investment trust's shares are worth more than its underlying assets, it is said to be trading at a premium; if they are worth less, it is trading at a discount. In theory, investment trusts that are trading at a discount are the most attractive for investors because of the likelihood that the discount will become smaller, thus making the investment worth more. If a discount of 20 per cent narrows to 10 per cent, the investment will be worth 10 per cent more. The bigger the discount, the better. But this is not always the case. More important is the investment trust's track record.

Investment trusts have been growing in popularity during the last few years. This is largely due to the efforts of the Association of Investment Trust Companies which has worked hard to have them put on the investment map. Quite often figures are bandied about that claim to show investment trusts beat unit trusts hands down when it comes to performance. In some cases this may be true, but some degree of caution is necessary.

Some of the top-performing investment trusts are heavily 'geared'. This means that the trust manager has borrowed money against the trust's assets and used it to buy more shares. This has the effect of exaggerating any movements up or down in the asset value of investment trust shares, and makes it more likely that the share value will also move up. This is all very well in a rising market, but if there is a slump, investors in heavily geared investment trusts will suffer more than those in lightly geared trusts.

There are many variations on the investment trust theme, and much depends on the individual terms of the trust. But one fairly recent creation is the split-level investment trust. With these the share capital is divided into two types: income shares and capital shares. One attracts all the income generated by the trust, and the other takes all the capital growth. This enables investors to mix and match shares according to their investment needs. If they are looking solely for income, they can buy the income shares;

if they simply want their capital to grow, they can buy the capital shares. Very often investors mix the two.

Having chosen an investment trust rather than a unit trust, there is, ironically, a chance that you will end up with a unit trust anyway. In recent years there has been a tendency for investment trusts to trade at a discount to their net asset value (as explained above). There are several ways in which this discount can be narrowed, and the most popular has been to convert the investment trust into a unit trust. Those holding shares in the trust will have them swapped for units representing the exact worth of that portion of the trust's underlying assets.

TAX EFFICIENT SAVINGS

For gay men who find it difficult to obtain life cover, tax efficient savings play a crucial role, especially when planning for retirement. There are a number of effective pension schemes on the market but, although there are exceptions (see Chapter 5 on pensions), these are often insurance-based. But a pension plan varies from other forms of investment only in the way it is taxed. Pension contributions are free of income tax, provided they are less than a certain percentage of net relevant earnings. For the current tax year this ranges from 17.5 per cent to 40 per cent, depending on your age (see p. 119). So if, as a gay man, you are robbed of this tax efficiency, what are the alternatives?

National Savings

The most basic form of tax efficient saving is to buy National Savings Certificates, which can be bought at your local post office. There are two types available, offering different levels of return. First are those providing a set rate of interest which accumulates over a five-year period and pays out a tax-free lump sum at the end. Second are index-linked certificates, which work in the same way but pay a varying rate of interest depending on the level of the Retail Prices Index. The RPI measures the current inflation rate in the UK economy.

Tessas

Tax Exempt Special Savings Accounts (TESSAs) are relatively new types of account offered by banks and building societies. Anyone over the age of eighteen can save up to £9000 in a TESSA and receive the interest free of all tax. Unfortunately this is the total allowance, and is not available every year. Up to £3000 can be saved during the first year. In any of the following years a maximum of £1800 can be deposited, until the upper limit of £9000 is reached. This amount cannot be increased by making deposits with different financial institutions.

Any taxpayers saving money in deposit accounts should consider switching to a TESSA. While deposits are a secure way of investing your money, the returns are usually lower than other, racier, types of investment. The tax advantages of a TESSA will help maximize returns.

Personal Equity Plans

These have been around since the beginning of 1987, but since those early days they have changed quite a bit. Originally they formed part of the Conservative government's strategy to encourage wider share ownership. Anyone over the age of eighteen could invest in UK shares without

paying either capital gains tax or income tax on the proceeds. It was an almighty flop. Instead of increasing share
ownership, all that happened was that those already holding shares shifted a portion of them into a PEP to reap the
tax-free benefits. Since then, PEPs have been expanded to
include a variety of investments.

Up to £9000 a year can be invested in PEPs. Of this,
£6000 can be put into a general PEP which invests in UK
company shares listed on the Stock Exchange or quoted on
the Unlisted Securities Market (USM). Alternatively,
the £6000 can be put into a unit trust or investment trust
provided at least 50 per cent of its assets is invested in
companies quoted on EC stock exchanges. (In spite of the
50 per cent rule, £1500 can be invested in overseas investment and unit trusts.) By opening up PEPs to pooled
investments in this way, their popularity has soared. The
most recent modification to PEPs is the single-company
PEP. With one of these you can invest a further £3000 per
year tax-free. This is especially attractive for employees who
benefit from share purchase schemes offered by the company that employs them. Aside from this, a certain amount
of caution is necessary when buying single-company PEPs.
Spreading your investments is the best way to mitigate
against the risk of having too high a proportion of your
savings in one area or company. If you buy one company's
shares to use up your single-company PEP allowance this
year, choose another company next year.

Apart from lump-sum investments, there are plenty of
PEP managers offering regular savings versions. So even
if you do not have a spare few thousand lying around
the house, PEPs can still be of use. The hardest part about
PEP investment is knowing which one to choose. Since

the government became more generous about what PEP investment should include, the number of managers offering them has mushroomed. Stockbrokers, insurance companies, unit trust companies – they all offer PEPs.

Very often, investors plump for any manager simply to ensure that they take advantage of all their tax-free allowances before the end of the year. But fear of missing out is far from the best way to select an investment. Possible tax advantages will rapidly pale into insignificance if the PEP manager fails to deliver the goods. Unfortunately, looking at past performance can be harder here than usual. Because of the range of investments PEPs include, it can be very difficult to work out how an individual PEP manager has performed.

With any PEP there are several potential pitfalls that need to be considered. One important thing to look at is the level of charges. These can include all the charges typical of the underlying unit trusts, investment trusts, and shares (initial charge, annual management charges, dealing costs) plus overall charges for the PEP itself. Clearly, if these become too heavy they can severely damage even fairly impressive investment returns. Luckily, because of the growing competition for PEP business, there are good deals to be found.

Another problem can arise if the PEP manager fails to convert your cash into the assets required under PEP rules. All PEP managers are allowed to hold cash on deposit for a while before it is properly invested. In the meantime it will attract interest gross of tax like any other PEP investment. But if the PEP is encashed without the money ever having found its way into an authorized PEP investment, investors will be liable to income tax based on their tax position in the year the gains are realized. For this reason, you need to clarify how quickly the PEP manager intends investing your cash.

When looking at PEPs as an alternative to insured pension schemes, there is one important factor to bear in mind. While pension contributions are made net of income tax, the benefits will be taxed as income according to your tax position after retirement. PEP contributions, if made from income, are made from earnings after tax. Depending on which tax band you fall into (and assuming that if you pay income tax at only 20 per cent you cannot afford to make a PEP investment), your PEP investment immediately starts at a 25 or 40 per cent disadvantage to normal pension contributions. Although the benefits will be paid free of all taxes, most PEPs will struggle to provide the same benefits as a good pension scheme. While PEPs are a way of making up some lost ground for those who cannot access insured pension schemes, they are very much a second choice.

Finally, there is also a political risk attached to PEPs: because they were created as part of a political strategy, there is a chance that at some future date they could be abolished. PEP managers tend to play this aspect down, insisting that even if PEPs were abolished it would not affect those already in existence. But the fact is that nobody knows for certain. Pensions, on the other hand, are far less likely to be adversely affected by future political change because all governments and administrations in the UK recognize the importance of encouraging individuals to provide for their retirement.

Enterprise Investment Schemes

Enterprise Investment Schemes (EISs) were announced in the 1993 Autumn Budget as a replacement for Business

Expansion Schemes (BESs), which were abolished on 1 January 1994. As with BESs, EISs are designed to encourage investment in new businesses but are slightly more restrictive, even though up to £100,000 can be invested in unquoted trading companies (those not listed on the Stock Exchange) in any one tax year compared with £40,000 for BESs. Instead of the former 40 per cent relief on money paid into BESs, money invested in an EIS attracts 20 per cent tax relief. That means that investment to the limit of £100,000 will actually cost the investor £80,000 (although investments made before April 1994 were limited to £40,000). Up to half the amount invested – to a maximum of £15,000 – can be offset against EIS tax relief unused by the investor from the previous tax year. Provided the investment is held for five years, any profit made on shares that are sold will be free of capital gains tax. If the shares show a loss, this can be offset against the investor's CGT or income tax liability.

In the 1993 Autumn Budget the Chancellor also proposed a new scheme for investors which is expected to be available from 1995. Venture Capital Trusts will be invested wholly in unquoted companies and all dividends and capital gains will be free of tax. Unlike EISs, investors in Venture Capital Trusts will not be investing directly in a single business. Instead their money will be pooled with other people's and invested in a range of companies. This makes venture capital investment available to smaller investors than would typically use an EIS, and helps reduce risk by covering a range of companies.

As attractive as these two types of investment may appear from a tax viewpoint, there is a proviso. Venture capital is money invested in new or very young companies that have yet to prove themselves. This makes it very risky. Without a successful track record, it is difficult for either professional or private investors to be certain of how such companies will fare in the future. No venture capital investment should be made with money you cannot afford to lose.

Offshore investment

Mention offshore investment, and some people will think of high-flying financiers looking for tax relief on their not so hard-earned cash, or dodgy wide-boys who can magically make your money disappear. While both these images are true up to a point, offshore investment is rather more mundane and user-friendly.

'Offshore' is simply anywhere which has a tax regime different from the UK's. The various countries that have become offshore investment centres are those where tax is generally lower than back home. From the Cayman Islands to Dublin and from Luxembourg to the Isle of Man, Jersey, or Guernsey, they all offer investors the chance to put money beyond the grasp of the Inland Revenue – at least for a while.

There are various ways of investing money offshore. Several of the savings plans and deposit accounts mentioned so far in this chapter have offshore equivalents. Many unit trust managers have offshore funds available which, apart from being based outside the UK, benefit from exactly the same management expertise. These are most likely to be used by people who spend all or most of their time outside the UK, for if they were to invest in typical UK unit trusts their gains would be subject to UK taxes. Anyone taking profit on any offshore investments while they are still officially UK residents will be treated for UK tax purposes in much the same way as if they had invested in an onshore fund. The main benefit for UK residents investing in off-shore funds will be reaped at such time as there is a change in their tax liability. They may plan to retire abroad, say, or they may currently be a higher-rate taxpayer who will become a basic-rate taxpayer after retirement.

There are a couple of risks associated with offshore investment beyond those taken by anyone investing in UK funds. If you invest mainly to gain tax benefits, there is always the chance these benefits will cease. Investment managers and the Inland Revenue are constantly playing a game of cat and mouse: as soon as one loophole is closed another one seems to open up. Numerous press reports have sounded the death-knell for certain types of offshore investment because the taxman has ended some benefit or other. Invariably there are other benefits available, and such funds continue pretty much unaffected. The tribulations of umbrella funds is one example of this.

Umbrella funds

An umbrella fund is one offering investors a range of sub-funds to invest in. The fund can either be managed by the investor or left to the fund manager. Either way, the client's cash can be moved quickly and cheaply between funds, both to spread the investment risk and to maximize the possible gains.

Although this type of fund is available in the UK, the offshore version has one distinct advantage: when money is moved from one sub-fund to another the investor effectively realizes a gain. Before the Inland Revenue tightened up the rules, such gains were liable to tax for UK umbrella fund investors, but not for those offshore. UK taxpayers investing in offshore umbrella funds would incur a liability only when they finally cashed in their investment. Very often they would time the final withdrawal of their cash to coincide with reduced tax liability in the UK or retirement abroad.

When the Chancellor announced in 1989 that all switches made between the sub-funds of offshore umbrella funds would be taxable in the UK, journalists predicted they would disappear. The investment industry denied this, and during the intervening years it has been vindicated. The big attraction for umbrella fund investors used to be a rollover tax break. When an investor switched investment between any of the funds offered by a particular manager, there would be no tax liability. This was different from the treatment of UK-based funds. If you cash in your investment in one fund, even if it is immediately reinvested in another fund, tax will be due on any gains your investment has made. With umbrella funds tax was due only when you finally cashed the fund in and took the money, and then only if you were still resident in the UK. Since the rollover tax break was ended, the number of umbrella funds has actually grown. This is because umbrellas were designed not for tax avoidance, but to maximize possible investment gains; the rollover tax break was added on almost as an afterthought. The benefits originally planned still exist. Switching within an umbrella fund is often cheaper than with the onshore equivalent. Also, because the same constraints on investment business do not necessarily apply abroad, offshore umbrellas can usually offer a wider range of sub-funds than is available in the UK – currency funds, for example.

The lesson here is that with all tax efficient investment the choice should not be made purely on the basis of tax benefits. When looking offshore, the same considerations apply. Always look at the performance of each fund. It may be that despite the tax advantages the performance of a UK unit trust outstrips that of an offshore fund.

Offshore banking

All of the UK high-street banks have branches in one or more offshore centres. Offshore bank accounts peaked in popularity a few years ago with investors who were not ordinarily liable for tax, for whatever reason. The problem at the time was that deposit accounts with banks and building societies in the UK automatically had deducted from them a special tax at source, called composite rate tax. Even those who were not liable to the tax found that they were unable to claim back the money they had lost. The only alternative was to open an offshore deposit account, often providing the same facilities as the customer would have found onshore, but with the added benefit of interest paid gross of tax.

Following the abolition of composite tax onshore, deposit accounts have also been able to pay interest gross of tax, and offshore accounts have become less popular. Now their main benefit is for those who want to have deposits in a currency other than sterling. Normally this would benefit someone who has liabilities in another currency: they may spend part of their year abroad, or keep a property somewhere that incurs foreign bills, for example. By keeping liabilities and assets in the same currency, you protect your money against possible currency fluctuation. Currencies within Europe are generally fairly stable, but the turmoil of the Exchange Rate Mechanism from late 1992 and through 1993 showed how easily problems can arise.

Offshore accounts can also offer cash-flow benefits to UK

taxpayers. If you are liable to UK income tax and have savings on deposit with a bank or building society, tax will normally be deducted from all your interest payments. Offshore accounts pay interest gross, regardless of your tax position in the UK. You will only have to pay tax on interest when such gains are realized. In the meantime, you can accumulate the interest and have it working for your benefit.

Whatever your reasons for wanting to invest offshore it is important to consider whatever regulatory controls there are on investors in the particular country you choose. Since 1986, UK investors have benefited from the Financial Services Act. This means that any investment product you buy from a company based in this country must be approved by the industry's regulatory body, the Securities and Investments Board (SIB). The FSA ensures that you will be compensated if you lose money because you were badly advised or cheated by an investment manager. But funds sold abroad are not necessarily protected by the FSA. Although some offshore funds are authorized by the SIB, there are many more which are not. Before handing over any money, make sure that the company you are dealing with is reputable. If possible opt for investments with SIB approval.

What investment?

Choosing between the various types of investment available depends on your individual circumstances and on the types of risk you are prepared to take with your money. Usually the answer is to bundle together several different investments to meet a wide range of requirements.

All of us need to have ready access to some of our money, just in case something unforeseen crops up. Here deposit accounts fit the bill. Money on deposit is safe and available as soon as you need it. If you make a withdrawal at very short notice the worst that can happen is that you lose a small portion of interest.

From here you can gradually move along a scale of risk and reward (and limited accessibility). Endowment policies with insurance companies will usually return more than a deposit account, and even if your initial investment does not grow very much it will at least not go down – provided you leave the money invested for a specified term, usually ten years or more.

Then you get into the area of stock market investment where your savings can go down as well as up. Whether investing in equities through unit trusts or investment trusts, or directly into the stock market, you should generally only use money you can afford to lose. Having said that, there are some guaranteed funds on the market promising to return at least 100 per cent of your original investment.

While there can be no hard and fast rules about where to put your money, everyone should start at the bottom end of the risk/reward scale. Depending on how far your money will go, you can gradually extend into the racier options where the rewards can be higher without risking complete financial ruin if the stock market crashes.

An important area not covered in this chapter is investing for one's own future. This is what we look at next – the world of pensions.

5
PENSIONS AND ANNUITIES

PENSIONS

Gay men are often more reluctant than heterosexuals to make private pension arrangements. This is because thinking about life after retirement inevitably brings with it the question of whether or not you will live that long. Confronting your own mortality against a backdrop of possible HIV infection can seem like a way of tempting fate. Many deal with their fear of infection by ignoring it. The fact is that most gay men will live to enjoy a long and healthy retirement, but a high proportion will have made little or no provision for it.

Putting some careful thought into how you will survive after you stop working, therefore, is absolutely essential. State retirement benefits are not enough. They are continually being eroded because the government simply cannot afford to stump up the sort of income people need to adequately fund their old age – or so they say.

The pensions revolution

The so-called pensions revolution was needed because of the changing population profile of the UK. State funded pension schemes which, until 1988, formed the backbone of most people's retirement planning, depended on there being a high proportion of people in work relative to those drawing their pension.

That situation is gradually being reversed in the UK and other developed nations, and some governments say it is more difficult to make ends meet. The rate at which the proportion of older people in the UK is increasing led to calls for dramatic changes in the way pensions are funded. The alternative, it was claimed, would have been a failure to pay the pensions people expected, or tax increases to cover the shortfall. As it happened, the Conservative government's free-market philosophy has fitted in well with the need to encourage people to make their own provision. This can be achieved in a number of ways, all of which attract beneficial tax treatment.

Making other pension arrangements, either through a company scheme or a personal pension, is essential. And the sooner you start, the better: the longer you have to build up a retirement fund, the bigger your pension will be. By starting early the cost of funding an adequate pension will take a much smaller portion of your income than if you start later.

For gay men the problem of how to fund their retirement is compounded by the high proportion of pension schemes run by insurance companies. Personal pensions, which may be based on life assurance products, could be especially problematic. If a salesman tries to persuade you to start a pension plan that includes an element of life cover, tell him to forget it. This may be a more tax efficient way of organizing a pension, but for gay men it will be fraught with problems. Even if you are only offered waiver-of-premium benefit (whereby the insurer undertakes to cover the premium payments on your pension if you become too ill to work), you need to make sure that this will not involve separate health or life cover. If it does, you could be asked to have an HIV test or end up on the Impaired Lives Register (see Chapter 7).

Expression of Wishes

Regardless of how you arrange your pension, whether through a company scheme or a private pension plan, it is important to complete an Expression of Wishes form. This is to make certain that if you die before you receive your pension, the full fund of money you have accrued to pay for it will pass to whoever you want to have it. On death, pension benefits from occupational pension schemes fall outside your estate, and will almost certainly end up with the wrong people if you do not make express wishes; there is even a risk that the insurance company will hang on to them. Pension benefits from a personal pension plan, however, are considered to be part of the deceased person's estate, so with these an Expression of Wishes form will be needed only if no will exists.

Although it is essential to take this precaution, the Expression of Wishes form can be overridden by the pension company. If you have asked that the fund be passed to your gay partner, the insurance company may decide that an ex-wife or child has prior claim. Even if no such relatives exist, the company may refuse to pay the fund to a same-sex partner. To overcome this, make sure you talk to an independent financial adviser who has successfully negotiated an agreement with a quality pension company whereby it will honour the express wishes of the insured.

State pensions

The most basic retirement provision is the state retirement or 'old-age' pension. Anyone who pays National Insurance (NI) contributions is entitled to one. State pensions are not geared to your own earnings during your working life, but – as a rule of thumb – are about 20 per cent of national average earnings. To qualify, you have to have been credited with NI contributions for about 90 per cent of your working life. That's why, during long periods of absence from work, you should if possible sign on as unemployed even if you do not need Income Support Benefit. If you register with the Department of Social Security, the necessary credits will continue to be made until you finally sign off.

The basic pension increases each year in line with the Retail Prices Index. Even if you make other arrangements, the basic pension should still be part of the picture. Your right to receive it is unaffected by other pensions you may have, and it can be a useful little extra when you decide to retire. Like other state pension benefits, it can be drawn in any EC country. So if you plan on retiring to Spain, your old-age pension could buy you the odd jug of sangria or the occasional face-pack.

SERPS

The State Earnings Related Pension Scheme, or SERPS, was introduced in 1978. Like the old-age pension, it aims to provide 20 per cent of average earnings. The difference is that this is 20 per cent of your own earnings, rather than 20 per cent of the national average. Entitlement is based on the level of NI contributions you have made and on an average of your income. For 1994/5 the NI lower and upper earnings limits are £56 and £420 a week; you pay NI at the rate of 9 per cent through the PAYE system.

It is this pension that the government says it is having trouble funding, as the percentage of income it is able to cover is gradually reducing. If you have paid NI contributions for most of your working life and will be retiring before 2009/10, you can expect to receive up to 25 per cent of your best 20 years' average earnings. After that year, the rate will be 20 per cent of how much you earned during your whole working life. This will deliver significantly less than the present system.

With SERPS, all you get is a regular income. None of it can be taken as a lump sum, and there is no way of getting to it before the normal retirement date. The height of its flexibility is in allowing you to draw it later: benefits can be delayed for up to five years, and will grow slightly during that time. Self-employed people have never been eligible for SERPS contributions or benefits, and have had to look to the private market to fund their retirement. The original private pension scheme, known as Section 226 contracts, formed the foundation on which personal pensions are based today.

PERSONAL PENSIONS

These old-style Section 226 'personal pensions' were around for a long time, and the modern day personal pension plans, sometimes referred to as PPPs, arrived as recently as 1988. Apart from filling the gap for those who were not otherwise covered by SERPS or by company schemes, personal pensions were introduced to encourage people to make their own pension provision. The government hoped that this would relieve the pressure on the state coffers, and that people would be a lot better off in retirement. NI contributions are not reduced, they are merely rebated unless you go into a company scheme. The contracting-out incentive for opting out is 1 per cent for people aged over thirty.

Personal pension plans are sold mainly by insurance companies, building societies, and banks. They are of a type known as money purchase schemes. Your contributions, limited to a stated maximum, are invested on your behalf in a tax-free fund. Over time the contributions build up, and – if the fund's manager is doing a good job – will have grown substantially by the time you retire, which with personal pensions can be anywhere between the ages of fifty and seventy-five. The money is then made available to fund your retirement.

The level of your pension contribution naturally depends on how well your investment grows. With personal pension plans there are three types of investment base, each with different levels of risk and reward. These are deposit administration, with-profits, and unit-linked plans.

Deposit administration

Deposit administration provides the same type of investment as any normal deposit account, but with the added personal pension tax advantages. Those opting for deposit-based plans tend to be people who settle for steady investment growth rather than risk losing any of their money in a more volatile investment. This is rarely the choice of younger investors. Instead, it is much more likely to be the base chosen by those who are already close to retirement who, unlike younger investors, do not have the years in front of them to make good any past investment mistakes.

With-profits

Next are with-profits contracts. With these, all regular and single contributions are invested in a life assurance company fund. These funds are extremely large and cautiously invested, making them less prone to the ups and downs of the various investment markets. Because this makes them a safer option than some other investments (such as unit trusts, investment trusts, and stocks and shares), they would ordinarily be expected to offer a more modest return. Even so, a few years ago, they were delivering annual returns in the form of bonuses of up to 20 per cent.

Unfortunately, things are changing – so much so that many finance industry observers wonder whether with-profits contracts will survive. In recent years the profits (bonuses) on such plans have been hit heavily by generally poor investment returns. It is now taking with-profits plans much longer to return an amount at least equal to the amount the investor pays in. Only 10 per cent of all such pensions over five years old are worth more than the amount of cash the investor has handed over to the pension company. This is clearly not a good option for those only a few years from retirement. But with-profits pensions are not the only 'safe' investments to be hit by falling returns. Building societies and bank deposits have also been offering lower returns, without so much as a murmur from the financial press. In fact, regardless of falling bonuses, with-profits funds usually return more money over, say, a ten-year term than do deposit accounts over the same period, while guaranteeing the safety of your capital investment and all accrued bonuses.

Unit-linked plans

Unit-linked pension plans (those invested in unit trusts) allow investors to choose from a number of different funds giving access to potentially huge returns from stocks and shares. The downside is that the risk of losing money is much higher than for many other types of investment. Unit-linked fund managers invest in a range of stocks and shares, gilts, and fixed-interest stock. (Gilts and fixed-interest stock are nearly all extremely secure investments offered by large companies or governments for a fixed term and with a fixed rate of return.)

Funds are often graded according to how risky they are. Investors who are happy to take bigger risks with their money for the chance of making bigger profits can always find a fund to suit their needs. Those investments are explained more fully in Chapter 4. Unlike deposit plans and, to an extent, with-profits plans, unit-linked invest-ments rarely offer capital guarantees. The money you pay in will buy a number of units whose value will rise and fall with the value of the underlying unit trusts. These in turn move up or down with the fortunes of the stock market.

So, although unit-linked pensions carry a higher risk of losing money, they are also more likely to give better returns than other types of personal pension. Historically, investment in the stock market has outpaced all other types in spite of the occasional slump. But those funding pensions from equity-based investments should ensure they have enough time left before retirement to overcome any difficult patches.

Switching

Some companies allow investors to switch between different investment bases rather than insisting that your pension fund is restricted to being on deposit, in a with-profits fund, or in a unit-linked plan. With such plans you can alter the type of investment over the course of your working life to suit your circumstances at the time. While you are younger, you could invest in a unit-linked personal pension. With time on your side you will be able to enjoy the hoped-for steady growth in equity prices, while still having time to overcome any stock market crashes.

Within a few years of retirement, or at any time when you expect the stock market to drop, you can switch into a safer with-profits fund or a deposit fund. With the new-style unitized with-profits funds on the market, this should be quite straightforward. (These are basically the same as the more typical with-profits funds, except that they are divided into units in the same way as unit trusts. This has no effect on the performance of the fund, but it does make it easier to move investments between with-profits and unit-linked funds.) Something to be wary of is that some schemes only allow you to make the move once from a unit-linked base to a with-profits or deposit fund. Once you have moved, that's where you have to stay. This is fine if you are close to retirement and simply want to consolidate gains you have made in a riskier investment environment. But for those just looking for a temporary haven, this restriction could be a disaster. A good adviser would never allow you to join a scheme like this.

Taking your 25 per cent cash benefit

Although, as a rule, fifty is the earliest age at which you can take your personal pension benefits, there are exceptions. With occupations from which people traditionally retire earlier – jockeys, models, footballers, and racing drivers, for example – the Inland Revenue allows benefits to be taken earlier. The same applies if you become too ill to work before retirement. It should be borne in mind, though, that the earlier you encash your pension plan, the smaller the benefits will be.

There are also legal restrictions on how the money can be used. At least 75 per cent of the fund should be used to buy an annuity (see p. 139). The other 25 per cent, as mentioned above, can be taken as a tax-free lump sum and can be spent as you wish. With an annuity, an insurance company agrees to pay a regular income in exchange for a lump-sum payment. The same companies that sell personal pension plans also usually sell annuities. It may be tempting to stick with the same company for both, but in fact it is better to shop around first.

The open market option

Since the arrival of the Financial Services Act in 1988, all personal pension contracts must include an open market option. This means that you are free to take your pension fund to whichever company will offer you the best income for it. This is because companies providing the highest investment returns for personal pension funds are not necessarily the best in the market for annuities. An independent adviser will be able to tell you which companies are currently offering the best deal. The maximum of 25 per cent of the fund that can be taken as a cash sum does not include the portion of the fund paid for by the DSS – commonly known as protected rights – nor does it include your basic old-age pension.

Contributions

A certain proportion of your salary is tax-free if you pay it into a personal pension. The proportion rises with age, as shown in the table. This concession makes a personal pension one of the most tax efficient ways of saving, but you cannot make contributions beyond the stipulated limits. Any contributions which you make in excess of the limits will be refunded to you net of tax.

Contributions made by employees to a personal pension are paid net of basic-rate tax under a scheme called Pension Relief At Source (PRAS). Those paying tax at the higher rate of 40 per cent must claim back the difference between the basic rate and the higher rate at the end of the tax year. Self-employed people pay the full pension and claim back their tax relief when submitting their annual Schedule D tax return.

Age	to 36	36–45	46–50	51–55	56–60	60+
Percentage	17.5	20	25	30	35	40

Percentage of earnings free of tax if paid into a personal pension depending on age.

As with other personal pension plan investors who were previously in company schemes, self-employed people can, if they wish, have any accrued money still held in their former employer's scheme transferred into their personal pension plan. Alternatively, they can transfer this money into something called a Section 32 buy-out bond. At least 40 per cent of transfers are still made through a Section 32 buy-out bond, as they guarantee the payment of a Guaranteed Minimum Pension (GMP) and may provide more tax-free cash on retirement. However, they are more complicated to set up and so many advisers shy away from them. Do check that your adviser is acting in your best interests rather than merely acting in the interests of simplicity.

The earnings cap

Apart from the maximum percentage of net relevant earnings from which contributions can be made, there is a maximum level of income from which tax-free pension contributions can be made. For 1994/5 this limit is £76,800. The earnings cap has been heavily criticized, the more so since it no longer appears to be moving up as quickly each year as was originally intended. The 1993 Autumn Budget increased the earnings cap for the first time in two years. Those earning much more than £76,800 and funding a personal pension will inevitably suffer a steeper drop in living standards after retirement than those on a lower income. There is, of course, nothing to stop you paying in more than the limit stipulates if you can afford to, but any such contributions will not attract tax relief. If you are lucky enough to be earning more than £76,800, you are better off using some other tax efficient savings scheme to bridge the gap.

Life cover

An additional 5 per cent of gross income can be used to fund a life assurance element within the personal pension. This can ensure that a lump sum is paid to your estate if you die before a given age, to a maximum of seventy-five. The inclusion of life assurance cover in a pension also means that contributions attract tax relief at the highest rate. For gay men, the business of life assurance may best be avoided (see Chapter 7).

Although opting for a pension without life cover could mean that you leave a gap in your financial plans, your pension can be arranged so as to ensure that your dependants benefit from the fund value if you die before you are due to retire. Without making this provision, your hard-earned contributions will stay in the insurance company's pocket. Your adviser will help you choose a plan which includes a return-of-fund option if you die before retirement. Be careful to avoid plans promising a return of contributions. These pay back only the exact amount of your contributions – possibly even eroding them further with previously hidden administration charges. In the meantime, the pension plan manager will have taken any profit your premiums had accrued. Return-of-fund will include any growth your premiums have enjoyed.

It is also important to make sure that this payment goes to the person for whom it is intended. If the pension plan manager will not allow you to make this clear on the contract, have it confirmed with a trust (see Chapter 1). That way you can make sure your partner or any dependants have the benefit of your cash, even if there is a likelihood of some infighting from hostile relatives about who is to receive your money.

COMPANY PENSIONS

Company pensions continue to exist in spite of the pensions revolution. There are two basic types: contracted-out money purchase schemes, and defined benefits schemes.

COMPSs

Contracted Out Money Purchase Schemes (COMPSs) operate in broadly the same way as personal pensions. An employer builds up tax-free savings on your behalf which, on the day you retire, will be used to buy an annuity. How much income you receive in retirement can only be guessed at when you first join such schemes. How good or bad it is depends on the investment skill of the pension fund manager and on the level of return annuities are offering at the time you retire. When you join a contracted-out scheme, you will give up any entitlement to SERPS benefits. Instead, you will acquire protected rights in a private scheme. Your old-age pension will continue as before. The main advantage with a COMPS is that your employer is obliged to make a contribution on your behalf, but he may insist that you also contribute. As an employee, you are entitled to put in up to 15 per cent of your salary. The incentive, apart from the use of the company pension as a perk to attract good employees, is a financial one. Contributions your employer makes are allowable against the company's corporate tax liability.

Unlike defined benefits schemes, an employer funding a COMPS is promising to maintain a certain level of contributions to your pension rather than guaranteeing a set income at retirement. This means, for the employer, that there is no need to worry about how well the pension fund is performing. In some cases employers can also use the pension fund for their own investment purposes, although this self-investment is restricted to 5 per cent of the fund.

Defined benefits

The more common occupational pension is known as a defined benefits scheme. Here the employee knows from the outset how much the pension entitlement will be: it is calculated as a proportion of the employee's final salary multiplied by the number of years of service. The difficulty some employers have in guaranteeing future benefits is beginning to cast doubts over the future of these schemes. Burdensome EC legislation has also aggravated the problem. As mentioned above, the proportion of final salary used by many schemes is typically 1/60, but it can be any fraction of final salary (see p. 125). The overall maximum pension payable under any defined benefits scheme is two-thirds of your final salary. Where benefits are based on 1/60 of final salary, it would need 40 years of service to reach the two-thirds limit.

The members of defined benefit schemes have tax-free contribution limits similar to those with personal pension plans. They can pay in up to 15 per cent of their net relevant earnings on qualifying income up to £76,800 a year. The difference, as with COMPSs, is that your employer is able to contribute an additional amount. There is no limit on the amount an employer can pay into the fund on your behalf. But no matter how much your boss contributes, the defined limits cannot be breached. There is, therefore, a possibility that the pension may become overfunded: that it will grow to be much bigger than is necessary to provide the pensions the company has promised its employees. If this happens, the employer may take a contributions 'holiday' until the surplus has been swallowed up. Alternatively, the Inland Revenue may decide to return the surplus to the company minus 40 per cent tax.

Clearly, contributions holidays are the preferred option. Numerous company schemes became overfunded thanks to the impressive investment performance of the 1980s. In some cases the fund became so big that employers have yet to begin making contributions again. A few employers decided to withdraw the surplus and use it in other cash-starved corners of their businesses. This brought into question the ownership of such funds. Do contributions belong to the company, or do they belong to the scheme members? The more powerful trade unions, faced with the prospect of seeing their pension funds rifled by bosses, complained that money originally allocated as an employee benefit should still be used as such. If anything, it was the employees who should be taking a contributions holiday or creaming off the surplus. Unfortunately, employers have rarely, if ever, shared this view. The consensus opinion is that employers are allowed to take the windfall returns created by the investment boom of the 1980s because it is they who will be expected to make up the difference if things go the other way. Beware, therefore, of 'Maxwell – The Return'.

Calculation of benefits

There are two alternative ways in which your final salary can be calculated in order to arrive at your defined benefits. (The Inland Revenue definition of final salary may differ from that of your employer. Before 1987 there were no caps on your final salary, but on all pension contributions made since then the maximum amount may vary. You should check the small print in your pension scheme booklet.) With the first, you can take your best year out of the last five before you retire, plus the average of any bonuses or commissions during your last three years of work. With the second, you take the average of your total income – including all bonuses and commissions – from any three consecutive years during the last ten that you worked. You choose whichever gives you the best pension.

As mentioned above, the limit on the amount of salary that can be considered for pension purposes depends on when exactly you joined the scheme. If you joined before 17 March 1987, your benefits were determined solely by your length of service with the company. For example, you could accrue the maximum pension benefit of two-thirds final salary (whatever that salary may have been) with just 10 years of service, and a maximum lump sum of one and a half times final salary with 20 years of service. With a scheme joined since then, you will need to clock up 20 years to qualify for the maximum two-thirds-of-salary pension, and 40 years for the maximum tax-free cash payout; there is a sliding scale for shorter periods of service. Anyone joining an occupational pension scheme between 18 March 1987 and 13 March 1989 had a salary cap of £100,000 for calculating the lump sum. In March 1989 the Chancellor introduced a harsher cap, which would increase annually in line with the RPI. Initially set at £60,000, for 1994/5 it is £76,800.

There is the option to take part of the pension as a lump sum, but as with the pension itself there are certain restrictions. The maximum lump sum that may be drawn on retirement is the greater of $3n/80$ (with n the number of years of service) times the final salary, and 2.25 times what the annual pension would be if no cash were taken. These restrictions apply to members who have joined a scheme since March 1989 and who are subject to the lower earnings cap. For those joining before then, different rules apply. For example, a scheme member who joined before March 1987 could, after just 20 years of service, draw a maximum lump sum of 1.5 times final salary.

If you have the option of taking a company pension, it clearly has its advantages. While you may otherwise persuade an employer to pay contributions on your behalf into a personal pension, these will not be allowed to exceed your personal contributions limit inclusive of your own contribution.

Death in service

A particular advantage for gay men is the death-in-service benefit the Inland Revenue allows pension schemes to pay. If you die before you are due to retire, a maximum of four times your final salary can be paid to your estate, together with a refund of all your personal contributions with interest. This is not subject to the typical restrictions life companies impose on gay men for life assurance. As a member of an occupational scheme offering these benefits you will be entitled to exactly the same treatment as your heterosexual colleagues. Better still, such schemes can continue paying up to two-thirds of your pension entitlement to any dependants. Whether or not you can have this directed towards your partner may depend on the wording of the scheme's contract.

Transfers

The main disadvantage with company schemes compared with personal pensions is their lack of portability. A personal pension is unaffected by job changes unless you move to pensionable employment. If you are in a company scheme, you need to be aware of how changing jobs may alter your pension entitlement. There are two alternatives to consider. The contributions and years of service you have put into a company scheme can be either frozen or transferred, depending on which suits your circumstances best. Much depends on the pension situation of your new job.

If you are moving to a non-pensionable occupation, you have several options: you can transfer the fund you have accrued in your former employer's scheme into a personal pension plan, leave it to accrue where it is, or transfer to a Section 32 buy-out scheme. Those who move to another pensionable scheme need to ascertain the benefit to them of transferring existing benefits to the new scheme. This depends on what benefits the new scheme will provide when the transfer is made. Some schemes will, for example, given you additional years' service in return for the transfer.

Every employer has to allow you to transfer your accrued pension rights if you want to, provided you have been a member of the scheme for two years or more and left service after 1 June 1986. In the past there have been examples of company schemes being awkward about providing a transfer value, but now they are compelled by law to do so. The transfer value will probably be subject to administration costs. These need to be examined closely to ensure they do not destroy the advantage of transferring in the first place. Transferring pension schemes is very complicated, and needs specialist advice.

Maxwell and the Goode Committee

The case of the Robert Maxwell employees who retired to find that their company pension funds had been 'borrowed' caused a public uproar. The Goode Committee, which was formed by Peter Lilley, the Secretary of State for Social Security, and chaired by Professor Goode, set out to make recommendations to restore public confidence in occupational pensions.

The Goode Committee recommended, among other things, that pension legislation be simplified and that legislation be introduced to clarify employers' obligations. The Committee also recommended that the valuation of company pension funds by actuaries be tightened up, with greater controls on the appointment of the pension fund trustees who are responsible for the investment of the funds. Additional restrictions on the future 'borrowing' of funds were also recommended, with a restriction on self-investment of company funds to 5 per cent.

Additional Voluntary Contributions

Far from overfunding their company pensions, most UK employees are contributing well below the amount they need to secure a full pension. Figures from the National Association of Pension Funds show that only 1 per cent of employees are contributing the maximum 15 per cent of their income permitted for company schemes. On average, employers deduct 5 or 6 per cent of employees' earnings to contribute to the fund. Those who want to put more in have to do so themselves by funding Additional Voluntary Contributions (AVCs). Unfortunately, people only seem to wake up to this idea when they are nearing retirement. Suddenly they panic about the amount of pension they are in line to receive, and desperately try to make up lost years of contributions. Consequently, the majority of people making AVCs are within five to ten years of retirement. There are signs that younger employees are beginning to make AVCs, but this is still very limited.

Only 10 per cent of employees are taking advantage of AVCs. Part of the problem in the past was caused by the rules governing them. They were originally designed to encourage people in company schemes to top up their pension contributions on a regular basis. If you took out an AVC at that time you had to keep up the same level of additional contributions for at least the next five years. This proved to be a discouragement for those who felt unable to make that sort of regular commitment. Since then the rules have changed, and it is now possible to make one-off lump-sum AVC payments. This gives you the opportunity of reviewing your finances towards the end of each tax year to see whether you can afford to top up your pension. Having done so, you are no longer obliged to do the same every year. The additional advantage of an AVC plan is that whereas company benefits are based on your final salary, non-pensionable benefits such as your car can be included as a relevant payment for the benefit of an AVC.

By law, every company scheme has to offer members an AVC option. But this does not mean that you have to stick with your own company's scheme. In 1987 the government introduced Free-Standing AVCs. These are offered by insurance companies and are independent of your company scheme. There are not many FSAVC providers, so scouring the market for the best deal is relatively easy. By comparing what your company offers with the terms available from other providers, you should be able to come up with the best option for you.

Those taking the FSAVC route have sometimes encountered resistance from the trustees of their own company's scheme. To take out an FSAVC, you need to prove to the Inland Revenue that your total pension contributions from both your company scheme and your FSAVC do not exceed the maximum 15 per cent of income. If your annual contribution to an FSAVC is less than £2400, this proof can be provided by showing wage slips, but anything above this figure has to be verified by the trustees of your company pension scheme. This can be problematic. Trustees have traditionally resented the idea of performing free administrative tasks for the benefit of their competitors. Consequently, such applications have at best been processed slowly, and at worst they have been ignored completely. Having said that, around 90 per cent of all FSAVCs are below the £2400 figure, so prevaricating trustees will not be a problem for most people. Unfortunately, the government has not increased this limit since it was introduced in the 1989 Budget. Thanks to inflation, the number of FSAVC members whose contributions exceed this amount is gradually increasing.

AVC or FSAVC?

The decision to top up your pension with either your employer's in-house AVC or to choose one of the FSAVCs available depends on a number of factors. Most important will be the different benefits offered by each plan and, in particular, the past investment performance of the manager. As always, this can only be a guide to future performance, not a guarantee. It is more than likely, though, that an investment manager who has consistently underperformed will not suddenly start hitting the big time. For those opting for the FSAVC route, there is the problem that only a few plans have been on the market for the past five years, so track records are short-term. For longer-term statistics, you need to look at the performance of the manager's other investments. There are other considerations too. For example, it is increasingly likely that all of us will change our jobs two or three times during our working lives, and those in occupations such as journalism or marketing may change jobs quite frequently. Although the accrued benefits of your AVC will be transferable along with the rest of your pension fund into a new scheme, an FSAVC is simply transported wherever you go.

Those deciding on the FSAVC route will find themselves facing a series of other choices. FSAVCs offer the same range of investment bases as personal pensions: with-profits, unit-linked, and deposit administration. Ultimately, your choice between AVC or FSAVC, as with any pensions decision, comes down to whichever scheme will offer you the best income when you retire.

Alternatives

For some people, the topping-up choice may not be between AVCs and the various FSAVCs, but between AVCs generally and Personal Equity Plans. PEPs, as explained in Chapter 4, offer some impressive tax breaks. As with AVCs and FSAVCs, profits made on PEP investment are free of income tax and capital gains tax. The difference, and this is what gives AVCs the edge, is that PEP contributions are made from income net of tax rather than gross. Depending on whether you are a higher-rate or a basic-rate taxpayer, your PEP starts at a 40 per cent or 25 per cent disadvantage to an AVC or FSAVC. Only the most exceptional fund manager could make up this difference with investment performance.

But there are two areas of topping-up where PEPs could be considered. One is if you have already used all your AVC entitlement and would like to increase your tax efficient retirement income further; the other is if you wish to improve your tax-free, cash lump sum on retirement. Sadly, no part of the AVC portion of a pension fund can be taken as a cash lump sum unless contributions began before 8 April 1987. So, for example, if your employer is paying only one-third of your salary into the company scheme, you can improve your future pension by making AVC or FSAVC contributions, but not your lump sum. PEPs, of course, can be taken as a tax-free lump sum. Those who are not already up to their £9000 PEP investment limit might therefore think about using it in this way.

HIGH NET WORTH

High net worth is personal finance jargon for well-off. There is no strict definition of high net worth, but if you are unsure whether it includes you then it probably doesn't. Those who are in this position have a further range of pension options open to them. These fall mainly into the self-administered category: instead of paying someone else to look after the investments in your pension fund, you can do it yourself.

Although there are no legal restrictions on how much money you should earn to have a self-administered pension, there are several practical obstacles. The first is that companies offering administration services for such schemes usually have their own limits on minimum investment.

Second, even if they did accept smaller contributions, they would be unable to spread them thinly enough to reduce the investment risk. On top of all this the transaction charges on smaller amounts will inevitably swallow up a large portion of profits on relatively small investments.

But for those who can afford to take this route, there are a number of benefits. The most important is that you can have complete control over the way your money is invested, instead of trusting to a fairly anonymous fund manager. Alternatively, you can select one or a number of managers of repute in the various areas you wish to invest in. In addition, you have the option of changing manager should you feel they are not doing their best. And, for people in business, self-administered pensions can be used as an integral part of your company's finances as well as your own. This means that even if you do not have the time or inclination to manage your pension investments personally, a self-administered scheme can still be the best choice.

Self-Invested Pension Plans

There are two types of self-invested plan, one for individuals and one for companies, much the same as for the standard schemes described above. Self-Invested Personal Pensions (SIPPs) are the individual version, and Small Self-Administered Schemes (SSASs) the company version. Each of these allows the investors to decide how the money they pay into the scheme will be invested.

Self-Invested Personal Pensions

With SIPPs, the limits on contributions are the same as with any other personal pension. The £76,800 earnings cap applies too. To build your SIPP fund, almost any investment can be included. There are, though, some notable exclusions: endowment policies, unlisted shares, commodities, foreign currency, residential property, and, for directors, shares in your own company. SIPPs are offered by a number of companies, any of which your financial adviser will happily put you in touch with.

For people in business or a partnership, SIPPs offer one particular advantage: your pension fund can be used to invest in commercial property. This can include property belonging to your company (a major exclusion is property owned by your company before the SIPP is started). New property can be bought by the pension fund and then rented to your company, leaving cash or other loan facilities available for further capital expansion. Any future increase in the value of the property will be free of tax once it becomes one of your pension fund's assets. The rent paid into the fund will, likewise, be free of tax, and will also be an allowable expense against corporation tax within your company.

There are only one or two disadvantages in doing this. Having your business's property tied in with your pension benefits could cause problems when you decide to retire, especially if this is earlier than expected – and it proves difficult to sell the property. If your company cannot afford to buy it, things can become complicated.

For those who are employees of a company rather than directors, the restriction on your own company's shares does not apply. Provided yours is a listed company, your SIPP can buy as many of its shares as you like. As with any pension fund investment, profits are free of all tax. The charges made by the SIPP manager vary depending on how much work there is to do. Even when the manager does nothing more than provide the legal framework, you will probably still incur certain charges. Individual charges will be made on particular deals where assets are either brought into or taken out of the scheme.

SIPPs that are run by an insurance company are sometimes slightly different from otherwise fully self-invested schemes. They are known as hybrid schemes. Part of the scheme has to be invested in the insurance company's own funds. Different companies make various demands about how big this level should be. The thing to bear in mind is that an insurer only allowing you to invest in its own fund is offering not a self-administered scheme, but a standard personal pension operating under a different name. Although having an insurance fund element may seem like a cop-out, it can be useful in reducing costs. Quite often several of the administration charges that would normally be charged separately are taken care of in the insurance element, and can make the SIPP cheaper than its fully self-invested rivals.

Small Self-Administered Schemes

Small Self-Administered Schemes (SSASs) are a type of executive pension plan (see p. 138). They provide pension benefits for the directors of small to medium-sized companies. The definition of how big or small a scheme should be is open to some interpretation. Generally, as far as the Inland Revenue is concerned, 'small' means up to 12 members. These members are simultaneously the scheme's beneficiaries and its trustees. In a self-administered scheme, the trustees are the ones who decide on the investment strategy of the fund. Some independence in investment choice is created by the requirement that every SSAS appoint a pensioner trustee. He or she can have no previous connection with either the company running the SSAS or the directors.

The pensioner trustee's job is to oversee the running of the SSAS and to ensure that it conforms with the Inland Revenue's requirements. Before the SSAS rules were updated, the pensioner trustee was relatively free to decide how much influence to exercise over the daily activities of the fund. But because of the high number of unsuitable investments the Inland Revenue was presented with, it later insisted that the pensioner trustee should become much more involved. This is not to suggest that pensioner trustees did not do their job, but clearly some were being less vigilant than others. If, for example, a pension fund bought a commercial property which the Inland Revenue eventually rejected as a permissible investment, the scheme would lose any tax advantage of the purchase and the incidental costs of purchase will have been for nothing. Such waste of time and money was a hindrance to the Inland Revenue as well as to the scheme. The current rules require the pensioner trustee to nip in the bud any unacceptable investments. Some of them have always taken a more hands-on approach, even to the extent of holding the scheme's chequebook to make sure every purchase is vetted. Ultimately they have no sanction over whether or not the scheme's members make an unsuitable investment, but few members would risk flying in the face of their advice.

SSASs have been the subject of a lot of ifs and buts from the Inland Revenue, and the rules governing them have been progressively tightened up. At one stage, many believed that they were being regulated out of existence. The main attraction for most companies with SSASs is the same as with SIPPs: the pension fund is free to buy the company's property and then rent it back.

As with their SIPP counterpart, there are both pure self-administered schemes and hybrids. And as with SIPPs the insured element of the scheme provides the administrative framework for the SSAS, including providing a pensioner trustee. Personal contributions to SSASs are restricted to the normal 15 per cent of income for the directors, plus the £76,800 earnings cap in the same way as anyone else contributing to a pension scheme.

SSAS benefits

There is a slightly strange twist to the way benefits are worked out. Even though SSASs are money purchase schemes, the pension the scheme members receive is restricted in the same way as with defined benefits schemes, although you can use an uplifted accrual rate of 1/30. This effectively puts a block on the amount of money the company can pay into the scheme on the directors' behalf. Unless the directors are careful, it would be very easy to overfund the scheme.

Apart from regular income SSAS members can also take a lump sum on retirement of one and a half times however much pension they receive. If any of the scheme members dies before they reach retirement, that person's portion of the fund will pass to their estate. For gay men it will be important to ensure that this money is directed in the way they want (see Chapter 1). Whoever you nominate to take the value of the fund will have to use it to buy an annuity (see p. 139). In this way the fund can be used for your gay partner's benefit to work in the same way as the traditional 'widow's' pension that many company schemes offer.

The risk with any money purchase scheme is that annuity rates may be low when you retire. If they are particularly below par and appear to have a good chance of rallying later, you can postpone taking your pension until later. The maximum time you can defer buying an annuity is five years. During that time you would expect annuities to have improved. In the meantime, while you are unable to cash your share of the SSAS, the pension you would otherwise expect to receive will be paid directly by the SSAS fund.

Executive pension plans

Executives and directors have several options open to them when making pension arrangements. Where no company scheme exists but the employer is prepared to make contributions, a personal pension plan seems an obvious choice. The 17.5 to 40 per cent of gross income that can be paid into a personal pension plan will provide a respectable pension.

Executives and directors have a slight advantage here. Although employee contributions into executive pension plans (EPPs) are restricted to 15 per cent of salary, there is no restriction on the amount your company can pay. Instead, a limit of two-thirds of final salary is placed on the eventual pension. This will also benefit directors who have chosen to take relatively small salaries, but are taking further income in the form of dividends from invested profits. While this arrangement will mean that a portion of the director's income will be free of NI deductions, the disadvantage is that the Inland Revenue will not include dividend income as part of your yearly salary. The final two-thirds salary received will then be smaller than if the full amount you received as payment were classed as salary.

With some EPPs, the members are able to act as the scheme's trustees. In other words, they are responsible for the way the fund is operated. For gay men in business this has the advantage of allowing them to decide the rules of the scheme, and makes it easier to ensure that gay partners are treated fairly. Trustees can also have control over how the fund is invested (as with SSASs, pp. 135–6).

ANNUITIES

Annuities are sold by life companies and provide a regular income in return for a lump-sum payment. Although anyone with available cash can buy an annuity, they are most commonly associated with money purchase pension schemes. With personal pension plans and some company pension schemes, the investor will be paid a lump sum when he or she dies. While up to 25 per cent of this can be used in whatever way the pensioner wants, the rest of it must be used to buy an annuity.

Insurance companies offering personal pension plans will also be able to offer you an annuity. But annuity rates vary, so before making your choice ask an independent financial adviser which companies are offering the best rates – the list may not include the company you bought your pension plan from.

There are several types of annuity, offering different benefits. One type may be better suited to your individual circumstances than another.

Immediate annuity

The basic type is an immediate annuity. You hand over your fund, and the insurance company agrees to pay you a set regular income for the rest of your life. The thing to bear in mind here is that annuities are the complete inverse of life assurance: the risk the insurer takes is not that you will die soon, but that you will live too long. The older and sicker you are, the better the insurance company likes it. It already has your money and if you pop your clogs sooner rather than later it will no longer have to pay out.

Right now you are probably thinking that here is an area of personal finance where gay men can beat insurance companies at their own game: if being gay is a disadvantage when you are buying life assurance, surely companies must be clamouring to sell gay men annuities at highly preferential rates? But, of course, this is not the case. It is indicative of the insurance companies' stance on HIV that their conviction of how deadly the disease is does not extend to annuity prices, even though the chief factors determining the cost of annuity are age and sex – not sexuality. Some companies will provide impaired life annuities. These types of policy will work out cheaper: the insurance company considers you to have a higher chance of an early death, which makes the contract cheaper for them as they are likely to have to pay out for fewer years.

So, the younger you are when you retire, the less income your money will buy. For money purchase schemes this causes a twofold problem if you decide to retire early. First, your fund will not have grown as much as it would have had you left it invested for longer. And second, the annuity you buy with this reduced amount will not bring in as much income as it would do if you were older, because it is likely to be paying income for longer. But if you take early retirement for health or any other reason, and can survive financially without cashing in your plan, you do not have to. You can leave it invested after retirement until you are seventy-five.

Guaranteed annuities

The different types of annuity on the market offer a range of benefits, and it is usually simple enough to find one that suits your needs. With a basic annuity the risk you take, having bought it, is that when you die all benefits stop. If you die soon after retirement the insurance company will be the chief beneficiary of all your hard-earned pension rights. To avoid this, when you retire you can buy a guaranteed annuity which promises to pay your pension for a set period – even if you die. The maximum guaranteed period is ten years. If you die within that time, all the remaining payments will be passed on to whoever you have chosen to benefit from your estate. In this instance, your partner can benefit from payments for the remainder of the ten-year period. If you are still alive when the guarantee period expires, the annuity will continue to be paid for the rest of your life in the same way as a basic immediate annuity.

Another way of ensuring you get out at least what you paid in is with a capital guaranteed annuity. These promise to continue paying benefits until at least the amount of your original investment has been paid out. If you die having received only part of the original pension fund, the balance is paid to your estate.

Index-linked annuities

A problem with any kind of fixed income is that it can very quickly be eroded by inflation. An average inflation rate of just 5 per cent can virtually halve the value of your pension in ten years. To avoid the prospect of becoming progressively poorer in retirement, you can buy an index-linked annuity. The amount of index linking varies, as does the way it is applied. Some will promise to increase the income each year by around 3 or 5 per cent, while others will add a predetermined percentage or the level of RPI in each year, depending on which is the lowest. This means that your initial income could be much lower, but at least it would gradually increase.

Deferred annuities

There are also deferred annuities: you pay in your money now, and payments begin at some later date. There are a number of circumstances where it might suit you to do this, but it is nearly always as part of a much broader financial plan. It could be that annuity rates are particularly high at a period when you are not ready to take the income. Or you may have the money to buy an annuity now, but prefer not to take the benefits until later: your tax position may be set to change in five years, for example. You could be planning to move abroad.

Tax

Although there are tax benefits attached to the way you build up your pension fund, you will be liable for income tax on income from your annuity. This can be mitigated in two ways. To begin with, you will continue to be entitled to personal tax allowances on your income even after you retire. Up to the age of sixty-five, this will be the same as for those still in employment. After sixty-five, tax-free earnings are enhanced by special age allowances. The maximum allowance for people between sixty-five and seventy-four during 1994/5 is £4200. For those over seventy-five, the maximum allowance is £4370. Unfortunately there is a downside, known as the 'age trap'. Because age allowance is supposed to help support pensioners on limited incomes, it is clawed back from those whose income exceeds £14,200. For every £2 by which your income exceeds this level, the tax-free allowance reduces by £1. So, if someone between the ages of sixty-five and seventy-four earned £15,000 during the tax year, the £800 by which the limit is breached will mean that the age allowance of £4200 will be reduced by £400 to £3800. All earnings over this amount will then be taxed at the basic income tax rate.

The second way income tax liability is reduced in retirement is by the way annuities are treated for tax purposes. A portion of whatever income you buy with your pension fund is deemed by the Inland Revenue to be part of your original investment. So this portion of your income is tax-free. Liability rests only with the part of your income considered to be the profit on your original investment. Even if you live long enough for your annuity to have paid back all of the initial capital, the Inland Revenue will continue to view part of your income as returned capital.

From pensions, which provide for us when we have retired from work, we now turn to health insurance, which provides for us during periods of illness or incapacity during our working life.

6

HEALTH

The 1993 Autumn Budget brought further cuts in health-care spending. The Chancellor announced that Statutory Sick Pay costs would no longer be reimbursed to large employers. Invalidity benefit was abolished to be replaced by a taxable incapacity benefit payable following a medical test that is more stringent than before. These cuts reflect a welfare funding crisis that has been building up for years. Growing pressures on resource-starved hospitals have also created huge waiting lists. Many non-urgent but painful ailments can now take years to be treated. Private health-care in the UK is not comprehensive enough to make those using it fully independent of the National Health Service, but for those who can afford them private plans can help to plug the gaps.

Gay men buying private health cover are not hamstrung by exactly the same problem as when they are buying life assurance (see Chapter 7), but unfortunately this does not necessarily make it any fairer or cheaper. While being gay does not always exclude you from being covered, it can complicate matters if you have to claim. As with life assurance companies, the huge mutual organizations dominating private healthcare insurance seem to believe that gay men are fully responsible for the spread of HIV. When trying to buy private medical insurance, they will probably be subjected to an intrusive lifestyle questionnaire similar to

the one used by life assurance companies. Having disco-
vered that you are gay, nine out of ten companies will insist
on your taking an HIV test. Depending on the result, you
may be offered health cover – possibly at an inflated price –
or turned down out of hand. However, being turned down
for health cover does not mean you should forget about it.
A good adviser will be able to find the one company in ten
that is more realistic about the HIV risk.

The existence of companies that will take you on is a
consequence of market forces. Competition among private
health insurers is growing steadily. Recently, some of the
bigger life assurance companies have launched products
they hope will break the market dominance of huge non-
profit organizations like BUPA. Allied Dunbar and Norwich
Union have both launched private medical plans. But
although the number of providers is increasing, demand has
actually dropped. According to healthcare analysts Laing
& Buisson, during the first two years of the 1990s the
number of people covered by private medical schemes fell
by 375,000. This is not what the private health sector was
promised in the late 1980s. The ethos of choice and self-
sufficiency promulgated by the Conservative government
suggested that more and more people would look to the
private sector for ways of plugging the gaps left by the ailing
NHS. Clearly, this has not happened. Although journalists
are apt to quote the UK's emotional attachment to the NHS
as the main reason why the private sector has failed to make
a bigger splash, the real reason has been the recession.

The vast majority of private health plans are funded by
employers as a perk. Because of this, the recession has had
two effects on the market. As businesses cut costs, employee
benefits were among the first victims. The high level of

business closures also meant that many company funded schemes simply disappeared. Now insurers are waking up to the massive potential of individually funded private health cover. As with all competition between businesses in the same sector, the effect is beneficial for consumers. Companies are now frequently offering more cover at better rates than ever before. There has also emerged a more realistic attitude to risk.

Unlike life assurance companies, private health specialists have rarely looked seriously at the types of risk they take. Traditionally, they have taken a very broad view of the likelihood of you becoming ill, and balancing that against the cost of the treatment or income benefit you are covered for. This led to all sorts of problems once the competition hotted up. Companies cut premiums dramatically in an attempt to make private health cover affordable for individuals. By taking on more risk, their claims experience grew and the premiums they collected proved insufficient to cover the cost. Private medical insurers panicked in much the same way as life assurance companies did. In a kneejerk response to their own failure to market products sensibly, private health insurers flailed around trying to prevent unhealthy clients from appearing on their books. Once again, fit and healthy gay men were victimized.

Corporate ignorance about HIV has been even more pronounced in the health insurance market than with life assurance. By the nature of the cover they offer, private health companies are unlikely to be hit by Aids claims even if they did cover for it. There are various types of health insurance (discussed in more detail below) which basically cover hospital costs or replace a portion of income if you become too ill to work. Very seldom do policies provide cover for long-term degenerative illness. The only policy offering this type of cover is long-term care insurance (see p. 164) – another import from the USA. These policies cover people after retirement, and have yet to make a big impact in the UK.

People who are HIV positive or who develop full-blown Aids are unlikely to need inpatient treatment, and unlikely to be declared unfit to work until a very late stage in the disease's progress. So unless an Aids sufferer is covered for outpatient treatment, the actual exposure of these massive companies to Aids claims is a mere bagatelle. It certainly is of less consequence than the foolhardy marketing mania that beset them in the late 1980s. But in spite of the facts, health companies reacted first by rooting out gay men and then by excluding cover for HIV claims. If you are HIV positive but your claim is in no way connected with HIV, your claim will probably be refused. A test pilot unable to work because of vertigo could have his permanent health policy made void if he is HIV positive and insured with the wrong company.

In part this approach may have been a matter of restoring business confidence by at least being seen to be doing something. It doubtless caused problems for gay men in company funded schemes who preferred not to come out at work. Now, again thanks to market forces, some companies are relenting. Although all but one insurer excludes cover for HIV-related illnesses, gay men generally suffer no greater prejudice now than any other private health policy-holder. But the importance of seeking good independent advice applies as strongly with health cover as it does with life assurance, for some companies are better at handling gay clients than others.

MEDICAL EXPENSES INSURANCE

Medical expenses insurance is the best known and most widely used type of cover. In return for a regular premium, you gain access to a range of private hospital services. Sometimes these services are owned by the insurance company, but mainly it just foots the bill. The main benefits of 'going private' instead of using the NHS are relatively quick treatment – which is especially important for the self-employed – and comfort.

There are many health conditions which, although not life-threatening, can be extremely painful or debilitating. Because most of these are considered non-urgent, they come way down the list of priorities within the hard-pressed NHS. Depending on the efficiency or funding of your local health authority, that could mean waiting years for an operation. By paying for private treatment the problem can invariably be sorted out in a matter of weeks. In addition, your accommodation may be more like a hotel than a hospital.

The types of policy available are many and varied, thanks mainly to increased competition for business. Apart from the need to find an insurer that is used to handling gay business, your choice of policy depends largely on how much cover you want. Private medical insurance is historically marketed through company schemes as an employee benefit. Because individuals are unable to take advantage of the same economy of scale available to companies, private medical insurance was usually restricted to either large groups or wealthy individuals.

That all began to change in the late 1980s as competition within the newly deregulated personal finance sector began to take off. Companies started exploring new avenues of business. Various companies are willing to take credit for being the first to enter the budget market; Prime Health was certainly one of the first to target the mass market. Until then, most policies offered full cover: if you needed an operation, all your hospital bills would be covered and you would receive additional cover for home nursing, journeys by ambulance, and much more besides. But a few insurers realized that by reducing the number of services available they could sell medical insurance at a price which even those on an average income could afford. Other companies quickly followed suit.

Broadly, the three types of medical expenses plan currently available are:

• traditional schemes offering a wide range of cover for most types of illness; these are the most expensive, and most commonly form part of employee benefit packages

• cheaper plans covering a limited range of inpatient treatment

• budget plans restricted to a small range of operations, typically those for which there are long NHS waiting lists.

Because these policies vary so much, it is important to look closely at what is on offer. Usually there is a range of premium charges on both comprehensive and budget plans. How much you pay depends mainly on the cost of the hospital you are likely to stay in. There can be up to five hospital charge bands, ranging from the most expensive (usually in London or other metropolitan areas), through the less expensive provincial hospitals, to the cheapest (usually general hospitals). This seems to give those living in rural areas a head start, but it can be a disadvantage. Those paying a lower premium may be unable to claim for some types of specialist treatment if it is available only at a hospital in a more expensive band than the one they are paying for. Some companies are less rigorous, and allow movement between the different hospital bands if it proves necessary.

One area of cost saving with private medical insurance, which gay men will probably find themselves excluded from, is family cover. Heterosexual couples and families can make pro rata cost savings by including more than one person on each policy. Even if a gay couple successfully persuaded an insurance company to offer them the same benefits as a heterosexual couple (and I have never heard of this happening), it would be highly unlikely that a gay couple with children would be regarded as one family. If one partner is the natural parent, though, they will probably be offered family cover for the real parent and up to two children. In all other respects gay men will be treated as individual clients.

Discounts

Most companies also offer discounts of various types regardless of which hospital band you select. If you opt to pay your premium yearly rather than monthly, companies will often reduce the total annual premium by between 5 and 20 per cent. If you would otherwise have this cash on deposit, this discount can work out to be very cost effective, depending on the rate of interest your money would have attracted. Some discounts will be higher than the interest offered by any building society or bank for money on deposit.

Other discounts are offered in the same way as for motor policies, with no-claims discounts and excess on claims. Those who are prepared to pay the first £100 or £150 of any claims can reduce premium costs by between 12.5 and 15 per cent. No-claims discounts are added to policies on a yearly basis – usually up to 50 per cent of the premium.

Some companies also offer a loyalty bonus whereby if you stick with them for several years, future premiums are reduced. Sometimes this can appear quite generous. After two years some premiums attract a 5 per cent discount; with one or two companies the sixth year of cover is free. The thing to check here is how the loyalty bonus compares with how standard premiums vary between companies. It is hardly worth paying an inflated standard premium for the sake of getting free cover later on. The same applies to non-smoker discounts. These are usually a marketing-friendly way of masking smoker penalties, and are not really a discount at all.

Added together, bonuses can shave a substantial amount off the cost of medical cover.

Maximum cover

When you have paid your premiums, some plans will cover all your private medical costs. Some insurers, however, place limits on the amount they will pay out. Almost all plans offer a full refund for the cost of hospital accommodation no matter how long you are in for. Such limits that exist are often expressed as a time limit, usually 26 weeks. In a few cases insurers impose a cash limit on claims depending on which hospital band you chose; this ranges from £200 to £500.

Drugs and dressings are also generally fully covered by the insurance company. Fees for surgeons and anaesthetists are more often limited. This does not mean that a surgeon will stop halfway through an operation if the money runs out, but you could be landed with a bill for anything not covered by your health plan. Luckily, about half the plans on the market refund these costs completely.

Where maximum cover does exist, it is determined mainly by guidelines set out by the British Medical Association. Occasionally the insurer quotes a cash limit; this can be as low as £200, but is more frequently somewhere between £2000 and £3000 per operation. The operation itself is rated on a scale from minor, through intermediate, major, and major plus, to complex. Again, more often than not insurers will cover the whole cost. The few policies with restricted cover for operations limit claims to between £2000 and £3000.

Only when you venture into the more peripheral areas of cover are you likely to encounter more restrictions. So with almost any policy you opt for, there is little chance of finding that you have to foot part of the bill yourself if there are any complications – until those complications arise. Not the sort of thing you want if your operation turns out to be more traumatic than you expected.

Things like home nursing and ambulance costs are generally restricted to a specific sum, although a minority of plans will offer a full refund here as well. The range of cover for home nursing is from around £600 to £1700. There are a few exceptions each side of this figure. Where a home nursing limit is quoted it is typically for around 13 weeks, but one or two policies offer only a couple of days. As with most types of cover these restrictions can vary depending on which hospital band you choose.

Ambulance costs nearly always have an upper cash limit of between £100 and £200. If you have private medical cover but decide to brave the NHS waiting list, some plans will pay a cash sum for every night you spend in an NHS bed. This averages around £50 a night, up to a maximum of £2500 to £3000. There is also a payment to cover the cost of hospital accommodation for parents whose children are admitted for inpatient treatment. Here the benefit is generally restricted to parents of children under nine years old, and is between £25 and £75 a night, up to a maximum of around £500 or 30 days.

A few plans are subject to an overall maximum cover for any treatment taken in a single year. Where this exists it tends to be higher for comprehensive plans than for budget plans. It is typically around £75,000 per insured person for comprehensive schemes, and between £10,000 and £40,000 for budget schemes.

It is important to look at the small print of a policy to see exactly what extra cover is provided. Sometimes this can be impressive. Very often insurance companies are prepared to let you go for treatment not necessarily recognized by the medical establishment: some provide cover for various alternative medicines plus treatment by chiropractors or osteopaths. More generally, it is possible to find policies covering dental work or ophthalmic charges, including eye tests. Some cover psychiatric treatment. Very often cover can be extended to include temporary foreign travel, which may entail a temporary increase in premium charges, depending on where you decide to go.

PERMANENT HEALTH INSURANCE

Permanent health insurance (PHI) is a less well-known form of health cover, but one which can form a central part of your personal financial planning. Unlike medical expenses insurance, PHI does not cover the cost of treatment but replaces a portion of your income if you become too ill to work.

There are several state benefits available to those who are unable to continue working, but these can often prove inadequate. The basic statutory sick pay is available for up to 28 weeks and is currently £46.95 per week for people whose earnings are between £54 and £184.89 a week, rising to £52.50 for those earning more than £184.89 a week. A PHI policy can boost this meagre benefit and maintain your living standards during periods of illness.

Although there are a few exceptions, it rarely matters what illness you have if you make a claim provided it prevents you from continuing in employment. Here, as with various other insurance policies, HIV is not covered. And, as with its exclusion elsewhere, this is a somewhat illogical underwriting decision on the part of insurance companies.

Those diagnosed HIV positive will continue to work for almost all of the time they are infected. It is only if the virus progresses into full-blown Aids that any disability may occur. By then it is unlikely to continue for a long time and, therefore, a policy replacing income will have a relatively limited risk exposure. None the less, if you are HIV positive the policy will usually be made void even if you break your back skiing.

Being gay will not prevent you from buying PHI, but the usual constraints apply: you may be asked to take an HIV

test or have your premiums loaded. Do not entertain the
idea of using any company suggesting either of these routes.
Because PHI policies will not pay out for anyone diagnosed
HIV positive – even if the illness is unrelated to the
infection – the company is running no risk at all. Any idea
that it should protect itself further with advance HIV
testing or inflated premiums is, therefore, an absurdity.

Your premium costs should be no higher than anyone
else's. Ironically, with PHI it is women who are most
heavily discriminated against. Premium rates with some
companies are higher for women than for men, regardless
of individuals' health. This was challenged in the UK courts
by a dentist called Jennifer Pinder. Having bought a series of
PHI policies from Friends Provident, she took the company
to court claiming that different premium rates for men and
women contravened the 1975 Sex Discrimination Act. The
court decided against her, and accepted Friends Provident's
defence that women are more likely to become ill than men.
Luckily not all insurance companies agree with Friends
Provident, and many now have equal premiums for men
and women.

Beyond the attitude of different companies to gay men,
there are several other considerations when selecting a PHI
plan. No PHI cover promises to replace all of your income.
Usually it covers 75 per cent of gross earnings, but there are
some plans offering only 66 per cent. PHI policies also only
provide cover until the normal retirement age, currently
sixty-five for men and sixty for women.

The relatively small take-up of individual PHI plans
suggests that only a small percentage of people believe that
there is any risk of them becoming seriously ill before they
retire. If the sales of PHI policies compared with life
assurance is anything to go by, people are clearly more

prepared to countenance the risk of death than the chances of becoming disabled before they reach retirement. Statistics for the UK compiled by permanent health companies show that the risk is higher than most people realize and certainly higher than the risk of HIV infection. In any one year an average of 80,000 men between the ages of twenty and sixty-five will die. During the same period 400,000 men will be unable to work for at least six months because of accident or illness. More than 200,000 of them will be too ill to work for at least three years, and a good proportion of these will never work again.

In some ways, PHI cover is more important than life cover. Although insurance companies discriminate against single men they are perennially frustrated at being unable to encourage more young people to take out policies. In spite of their public declarations, companies are aware that a young insurance portfolio is less risky than an old one. But a young man with no financial dependants, also aware that he is unlikely to die for some time, can see no reason for buying life assurance. The most he could need, theoretically, is around £1000 worth of cover to pay for a funeral; if he has any outstanding loans these will also need to be covered. If he becomes too ill to work, the same young man effectively becomes his own dependant. Without insurance cover it would be impossible to maintain all but the most frugal of lifestyles. State benefits are bound to be unequal to the task. A good PHI policy will alleviate coping with the disability and prevent a dramatic fall in standard of living.

Choosing PHI

Making sure that the policy is a good one is the difficult part. The most important thing to consider is the policy's definition of disability. Since PHI first appeared on the UK market, some companies have tightened this up. Undoubtably the fairest is one where a claim is made if the client is no longer able to continue working in his present occupation or any other to which he is suited by training or experience. Others can be much more stringent, limiting claims to only the severest disabilities.

It is also worth asking your financial adviser about the claims track record of particular companies. PHI has been a loss-maker for some companies and they have occasionally reacted by disallowing claims that were already being made. There are cases where PHI companies have insisted that claimants are examined by a company-appointed doctor, whose opinion may be that the claimant is in fact fit for work, whereupon the claim was disallowed. Your adviser should have an idea which companies have attempted to reduce claims in this way. Although these types of experience are bound to make potential clients feel uneasy about buying PHI policies, there are still plenty of worthy companies about. The essential thing is to make the right choice at the outset.

The next consideration is how much cover the policy provides. Although most companies claim to replace 75 per cent of your salary (less state benefits and other income), there are some that have an overall maximum. If you are currently earning £50,000 a year, a policy with a £20,000 per year maximum will be woefully inadequate. Ceilings companies impose on the level of claims, if they change at all, will most probably move upwards more slowly than incremental increases in your earnings. So having bought your PHI policy, the disparity between your salary and how much the policy will replace will gradually increase.

A few companies, while not stipulating an overall maximum, will grade the percentage of salary they will replace according to how much you earn. They may pay 75 per cent of salary up to £30,000, but reduce this by half for any earnings above that figure. This may not be so important for someone whose cost of living falls well short of their salary. But most people raise their living standards to match their income, and few would find such an arrangement suitable.

As long as the policy covers you if you are unable to work, and it has a sufficient initial level of cover which increases annually by 5 per cent or according to the RPI – you are home and dry. One word of warning: buying a series of policies from a number of companies would not increase benefits beyond 75 per cent of salary if you make a claim. Any income you receive, no matter what the source, will be deducted from the 75 per cent total.

Premium cost

The premium cost of PHI plans varies widely between companies. Even within a particular plan, costs can vary according to what level of cover you choose. All PHI plans offer a range of deferment periods. This is a period of weeks following the time a claimant becomes unable to work where no money will be paid. At first sight this seems a bit strange, but in fact it can be very useful. The range of deferment periods can be anything from four to 104 weeks, and the longer the deferment period, the lower the premium. Which period you opt for will depend largely on your employment conditions.

If you are employed and have been with the same company for a while your employer will probably cover all or part of your salary for a limited time. There may also be specific earnings related benefits temporarily available. If your PHI policy pays out immediately, all this income will be deducted from the 75 per cent total of your claim. It may mean that you receive nothing from the insurance company at all until these initial benefits are used up. Before choosing a deferment period check with your employer to find out what sickness benefits you would be paid. You may even find that you are already covered under a group PHI scheme paid for by your company. If there are no benefits, or if you are self-employed, the chances are you will want to pick the shortest possible deferment period. Here it is important to match the premium cost of the policy with your likelihood of surviving financially for several months.

Premium costs will also vary with the term of the policy. This is a fairly recent trend. A few years ago, all PHI plans continued either for as long as you paid the premiums or until your expected retirement date. This has changed recently with the introduction of short-term plans. For insurance companies this offers the dual advantage of bringing premium rates down to a more affordable level, and helping them to capitalize on the younger, healthier end of the market. But there are advantages here for the client too. As we have already seen with other forms of insurance, an individual's insurance needs can change at various times in his or her life. The 'permanent' in PHI means that once a policy is started it cannot be cancelled by the company – no matter how your health or lifestyle changes – provided you continue paying the premium. That inevitably increases the company's liability and inflates the premium. Some companies are now offering shorter-term policies which are cheaper than traditional PHI plans. If you are at a time of your life when it is especially important to protect your income (you may have young children or particular financial liabilities), it may be preferable to opt for a short-term plan.

Not so pleasant is a trend towards reviewable and renewable plans. This is also a result of the increasing reluctance of companies to tie themselves into long-term contracts. Some companies now reserve the right to reconsider the conditions of your policy at various points during the term. If your health has deteriorated or you have become a professional mountaineer since you took out your PHI plan, the company will increase your premium or cancel the policy. Although this is not in the spirit of the 'permanence' PHI policies promise, it is an inevitable consequence of the financial problems insurance companies have faced in recent years.

In some ways, the variation of premiums from one PHI provider to another has no rhyme or reason. Big savings can be made simply by shopping around: even an identical policy can vary dramatically in price. The most expensive policies are generally those which include an investment element. With many plans the premiums you pay are simply swallowed up by the insurance company if you never make a claim. Since the majority of people are unlikely to claim, this seems a terrible waste. By paying into a plan which includes a portion of investment you will receive a tax-free payment at the end of the term, regardless of whether or not you have made a claim.

How much such plans return depends on several factors. First, as with all investments, there is the investment skill of the company's fund managers. Next is the level of charges the company imposes: if this is high it can rapidly erode even relatively good investment performance. Finally, some plans allow the policyholder to fix the expected level of return. This could fall anywhere between funding for a return equal to the total premium outlay to showing a healthy tax-free profit. A lot depends on how much you are willing to put into a PHI policy: the bigger the projected return, the higher the premium.

Extra benefits

Other benefits, which may also have an effect on the premium level, only come to the fore after a claim is made. One important feature of many policies is waiver-of-premium benefit. Unlike premiums on life assurance policies, PHI premiums do not stop after a claim is made unless the policy includes a waiver: the premium cost will still have to be met in spite of the claimant's reduced financial circumstances.

One point to be wary of, even if waiver of premium is offered as a benefit, is that the conditions of the waiver will not necessarily be the same as the contract itself. In particular, the waiver may carry a different deferment period to the main contract. Ideally the waiver should begin as soon as the claim is made. If you have no alternative sickness benefits and, for example, you have chosen not to have a deferment period, you do not want to find that a two-year deferment is automatically attached to the waiver-of-premium benefit. With index-linked policies, where the premium and benefits increase by a percentage each year, you should make sure that the waiver-of-premium benefit keeps pace with the actual premium cost. Otherwise, if you have to make a claim several years into the policy's term, you may find that the waiver of premium no longer covers the whole amount.

Index linking is another important point to consider. It may seem, in these times of relatively low inflation, that increasing policy benefits is hardly worth the money and effort. In fact, even low inflation can have a dramatic effect on the value of a policy over long periods. With policies that provide automatic index linking, the premium and benefits are increased each year by a predetermined amount. If you feel this is not enough you can usually increase it further. More importantly, some PHI plans allow you to increase the premium and benefits after a claim has been made. This is clearly important. It means that even while payments are being made, you will not be forced to sit idly by while a sudden bout of raging inflation eats into your PHI benefits. Understandably there are limits to how much you can increase a policy in this way.

A large number of PHI plans offer proportional benefits. If you are no longer able to continue with the previous job because of an accident or illness, but decide to take another, less well-paid position, a policy with proportional benefits will make up the difference between your new salary and the amount the policy covers you for.

Rehabilitation benefit is much the same thing, except that it applies to those who return to their old job on a part-time basis. While you are getting back into the swing of things following an illness, PHI will cover the reduction in salary. The only drawback is that some rehabilitation benefit is offered for a shorter period than the policy proper, so there is a risk of the benefit expiring before the PHI policy term is finished.

Exclusions

General exclusions under both PHI and medical expenses insurance include illnesses caused by alcoholism, drug addiction, self-inflicted injury, or childbirth. Certain dangerous occupations may also be excluded or subject to special terms.

A difficulty arises with all health insurance if the person applying for it has a pre-existing illness. HIV will disqualify you from cover, as will a range of other illnesses. Some insurers are prepared to offer a moratorium with certain illnesses: if you have not needed treatment for five years or so, you may effectively be granted a clean bill of health. The only proviso is that for two years the pre-existing illness, and anything related to it, will not be covered. The difficulty here is in defining which illnesses are connected. If you had a heart attack six years ago an insurer may happily provide cover, but with an exclusion for heart disease during the first two years of the policy term. But if during the first two years you make a claim because of high blood pressure, this could well be deemed to be related to your pre-existing illness and the claim disallowed.

If you have a history of illness and an insurance company agrees to a moratorium, it is important to find out what types of claim the company would consider as related to your previous health problems. You do not want to wait until you have a claim to find that the insurance company will not pay out.

Accident and sickness

Accident and sickness insurance is in some ways similar to PHI. The main difference is that the policy is renewed every year, which makes it generally less attractive than PHI. If your health deteriorates or you make a claim the insurance company can alter the terms of the contract at the renewal date. They may increase the premium, or even cancel the policy completely. Accident and sickness insurance, unlike

PHI, can be arranged to provide a specific amount of cover. The premium cost can be weighed against the amount of insurance you need. As with PHI, the benefits can be deferred for a while, reducing the premium cost further.

Long-term care

Long-term care insurance is a newcomer to the UK market. For health insurers it creates the final link in a chain giving people the chance to cover themselves against illness from the cradle to the grave. Long-term care covers the cost of residential and nursing treatment for elderly people – mainly considered to be those over normal retirement age. Insurance companies are increasingly selling it as part of a comprehensive healthcare package, but it has yet to make much of an impact in the UK.

Critical illness insurance

Critical illness insurance (sometimes known as 'dread disease insurance') is yet another health insurance option. Once you have taken out such a policy, if you go down with one or more of a range of specified illnesses the policy will pay you a lump sum. This money is tax-free and can be put to whatever use you choose. It can supplement income while you recuperate. If the illness means that your home has to be adapted in some way to make life easier, the money can be used for that. The types of illness covered are pretty much the same with most of the insurance companies selling critical illness benefit. The list normally includes heart attacks, cancer, renal failure, heart bypass surgery, strokes, organ transplants and several others.

The problem for gay men thinking of buying this type of insurance is that it is invariably attached to a life assurance policy. If you have problems buying life cover, you will be confronted by the same obstacles when buying critical illness insurance, even though critical illness cover rarely includes HIV. Astonishingly, the one or two insurance companies that consider HIV to be a critical illness will pay up only if you can prove that the infection was the result of a 'needle-stick injury' (an accidental jab with an HIV-infected syringe, usually affecting doctors and nurses). Again, it is important to find out from an independent adviser which companies have a better attitude than others towards gay men.

The relatively small number of insurance companies selling critical illness cover has its disadvantages and its advantages. On the one hand there are few providers to choose from, and therefore little competitive pressure under which the terms of critical illness policies might be liberalized. On the other hand, the main advantage is that it is not too difficult to survey the entire market.

Aids as a critical illness

Remarkably, critical illness insurance is the only area of the personal insurance market where cover against Aids is available. At least one provider includes the disease on its list. Unfortunately, a claim can only be made under limited circumstances: the infection must have been contracted through no fault of your own, and several other people must have been infected at the same time. This aims to discount all but those infected by blood transfusion, but with updated blood screening techniques this is now an unlikely event.

The wording of such policies is to a certain extent open to interpretation, though, and it would be interesting to see whether there are circumstances where sexually transmitted HIV between willing partners could result in a claim. Rest assured that if it did, such policies would disappear overnight. If you do buy critical illness cover there are two points to be wary of in addition to the warnings about buying life cover outlined in Chapter 7.

Illness definitions

It is important to be clear about what the insurance company's definition of each critical illness is. Although the sales literature may promise to pay out if you develop cancer, the policy wording may restrict this cover to certain types. For example, it may have to be life-threatening. This points up another of those grey areas where insurance companies may try and worm their way out of paying a claim in spite of taking all your premiums. Is a life-threatening cancer one you necessarily die from, or can it be a life threatening one for which you were successfully treated and saved? If critical illness benefit is paid only to cover a brief period between becoming ill with a fatal disease and dying from it, such an insurance policy is of little use. Notwithstanding the problems gay men face in obtaining them, there are basic life assurance policies which do the same job but more cheaply, by paying out benefits early to policyholders diagnosed as terminally ill.

This brings us to the second point to be wary of with critical illness cover. Where critical illness cover forms part of a life assurance policy, you should make certain that any future critical illness claims are not simply an advance payment of life cover. With payments for survivable diseases, this could cause problems: if, for example, you have a heart attack, there is statistically a good chance that you will make a complete recovery. With critical illness cover you will have received a tax-free payment that helped you financially during those difficult months. But if the money you received was in lieu of your life assurance, what will happen when you finally die? There will be no money available to look after your dependants. If you try to take out life cover after suffering a serious illness, the chances are that you will be turned down out of hand or forced to pay extortionately high premiums. For this reason the best type of critical illness benefit is one which leaves your life cover intact if you make a claim under the critical illness provision. That way, your financial provisions for the welfare of your dependants after you die will remain intact.

Tax treatment

The tax treatment of health insurance has caused considerable debate in the last few years. Because tax-free benefits are a powerful marketing tool, private health insurers have been keen to get the Inland Revenue on their side. Their argument in favour of tax relief is that, by encouraging individuals to make their own healthcare arrangements, pressure on the NHS would be much relieved. The government saw the logic of this, but only up to a point. Since April 1990 people over the age of sixty have been able to claim tax relief on premiums paid into medical expenses insurance. Basic-rate relief is claimed directly by the insurer, so those who are eligible pay only the reduced premiums. The interesting point to note is that it is the person paying the premium who is eligible for tax relief, and not the policy's beneficiary. Nor does the person paying the premium need to be related to the policyholder. The premium may even be paid by an employer as a perk. Here, though, the tax relief could be claimed only if the premium were not otherwise used to reduce the company's total taxable profits.

Medical policies qualifying for tax relief are those reimbursing private medical expenses. No minimum level of cover is demanded, so most UK medical expenses policies qualify whether they are comprehensive, budget plans, or those covering waiting-list ailments. The only exclusion is for policies covering cosmetic surgery, dentistry, eye tests, and private GP visits. If your policy includes any of these benefits, tax relief is not payable.

The small amount of tax relief available does not extend to policies where income is replaced, so PHI policies are excluded. But there are some tax benefits attached to PHI. Although individuals cannot offset PHI premiums against tax, premiums paid via a company might be tax deductible. So if an employer takes out a PHI policy as an employee benefit, the premiums may be deductible against company profits if cover is offered to a significant part or all of the workforce.

With either private or group PHI, any claims payments are liable for tax under Schedule D. There is, however, a tax holiday of one full year before any tax is levied. So if you happened to make a claim on 6 April 1994 – just one day into the new tax year – no tax would be due until 5 April 1996, effectively giving the claimant two years' tax-free income. Clearly, nobody can choose the best time to be sick or injured, but there may be circumstances where it would be financially beneficial to postpone a claim if it falls close to the end of a tax year. All PHI benefits are paid gross, so it is up to the claimant to ensure that any tax due is paid.

7

LIFE ASSURANCE

Most gay men and women do not need life assurance. Unless you have children or a financially dependent partner, or are after a mortgage or in business, you are better off without it. A salesman may claim that life assurance is so cheap you may as well have it. Even if it only costs you £15 a month, though, there are much better things to be spending your money on.

But for gay people unable to sidestep the need for life cover, sound advice is indispensable. While a heterosexual runs the risk of simply getting a bad deal if he makes the wrong choice of policy, gay men have much more at stake. At best they could end up paying a 250 per cent higher premium than a heterosexual man of the same age and health. At worst they could be refused insurance completely and find themselves on the Impaired Lives Register – the UK insurance industry's blacklist. Most people on it are one gasp away from breathing their last, and no insurer would willingly touch them with a barge-pole.

The HIV risk is the reason extremely fit and healthy gay men are frequently blacklisted. It doesn't matter that you have a negative HIV test, are monogamous, practise safe sex, or are celibate – insurance companies would rather you stayed away from them. Things have improved lately following a test case against Allied Dunbar in which a gay man succeeded in having his name removed from the Impaired

Lives Register. But in spite of this precedent, gay names are still being added to it. Once there, it is very difficult to have your name removed. If you have been refused life cover without good reason, it may be as well to see whether or not you are included. You can do this by contacting the Association of British Insurers at 51 Gresham Street, London EC2V 7HQ.

Although insurers feel that avoiding gays makes rather good sense, it is worth considering the following statistics, from Action on Smoking and Health. In the UK during the last ten years, 1,100,000 people have died from smoking-related illnesses. One in three smokers dies of a smoking-related disease; of these, half die before they are seventy. Less than 20,000 people have ever been diagnosed HIV positive, and only a fraction of them have died from Aids during the same period. Even accounting for the relatively short time for which HIV has been around makes a nonsense of the way gay men are treated by insurance companies. Yet if you are a smoker who otherwise appears fit and healthy, your heavily increased risk of dying young will add only a few pence to the cost of your life assurance policy.

The HIV risk provided an enormous financial windfall for insurance companies. Life assurance premiums were increased by 50 per cent on all new life policies – not once, but twice. Increased premiums are still pouring into insurance company coffers to cover a risk which the industry refuses to reassess. Whatever exposure it really had to HIV has supposedly been taken care of by sifting out gay men. If that's true, why have premiums not been reduced? And why are lesbians charged the same insurance rates as heterosexuals when they are at the lowest end of the HIV risk scale?

The reaction of the UK insurance industry to the HIV risk, and the way it laid responsibility for the potential spread of the disease squarely at the door of gay men, might ordinarily have breached the Unfair Contracts (Terms) Act, but the government was persuaded to exclude insurance policies from the Act.

The arrival of genetic underwriting is a further development likely to be used by insurance companies to isolate gay men. Scientists are now able to identify the genetic characteristics of those prone to certain types of illness. Babies can be genetically tested to find out what health problems they may develop as adults. Insurers are keen to use this new technology as a way of reducing risk further and boosting their profits.

What this frighteningly Big Brother-like move threatens is the creation of a two-tier society: the insurable and the uninsurable. Ironically, under these circumstances, if you were able to buy insurance there would be no point in doing so, for getting the go-ahead from an insurance company would mean that they had eradicated any risk. Here it becomes more sinister. Insurance companies will want to keep genetic test results to themselves; the only indication you may have of any problems will be when your proposal form is sent back. Only government action can prevent insurers from enshrining their social prejudices in the jargon of new technology. On past experience, this is unlikely to happen.

But despite the pitfalls, most people need to have some degree of life cover at certain stages in their life. With a certain amount of caution, gay men can find a way through the problem.

The principle behind life assurance is straightforward. Policyholders pay premiums into a common fund. This money is invested to increase its value further. The fund will then pay out a cash sum to the beneficiaries of those who die. From here on it becomes much more complicated.

Whole-of-life assurance

This is the most basic type of life assurance, and is most commonly used to plan for inheritance tax, or death duty as it used to be called (see Chapter 2). In return for a set premium, the insurance company agrees to pay out a lump sum when you die. Unless you cancel the contract or stop paying the premium, it will continue for the rest of your life. It doesn't matter if your health deteriorates or you develop a wild and dangerous lifestyle in later life – the insurer must honour the contract. In insurance jargon, this is the principle of 'utmost good faith'.

Provided you answered the questions honestly when you bought the insurance, the insurer cannot cancel it later. The most common whole-of-life policy is the with-profits contract. With this you take a share in the investment performance of the policy's underlying insurance fund. If the fund is doing well, the company will add bonuses to the sum assured. So £50,000 of life cover you buy this year should grow steadily each year as a hedge against inflation. The level of bonuses depends on how well the fund is managed. During the last few years insurance companies have struggled to maintain investment performance and have drastically reduced the level of bonuses they pay. Some have even paid none at all. Things may now be changing as insurance companies move towards renewed profitability.

There are two types of bonus: reversionary and terminal. Reversionary bonuses are declared each year. Once they are added to your policy, the insurance company cannot take them away. Terminal bonuses are added when the contract finishes or when the policy is surrendered. With a whole-of-life policy this happens when the policyholder dies. The way the total gains on a policy divide between reversionary and terminal bonuses varies between companies. Some pay larger annual amounts, while others add most of the profits at the very end.

When you buy a with-profits policy the insurer will usually present you with a prediction of the way the policy should grow over time. Since the arrival of the 1986 Financial Services Act, companies are prevented from making wild claims about how their policies will grow. But it should be borne in mind that the investment performance of companies varies considerably, so it is important to look at their track records before making a choice. This, of course, can only offer a rough guide, and there is no guarantee that a company with a good investment track record will continue performing well in the future.

Another consideration should be the proportions in which the company declares its bonuses. A company that delivers most of its bonuses as terminal bonuses will be a riskier bet than one delivering mainly reversionary bonuses. Because the level of terminal bonus is based on the performance of the insurance fund during the final year of the contract, there is a risk that if the fund performance takes a dive then so too will the value of your policy. Making sure that you die in a year when the fund performs well could be tricky.

Non-profit whole-of-life policies operate on basically the same principle as with-profits contracts but without the benefit of added bonuses. The amount of cover you have on the day the policy starts will be the amount paid to your estate after you die. These policies are generally cheaper than their with-profits counterparts, but apart from that they offer no clear advantage. They have specific uses for some types of tax planning, but even then, independent advisers will usually come up with a more effective alternative.

Flexible whole-of-life

The ultimate form of whole-of-life insurance is the recently introduced flexible, or universal, life policy. Unlike most basic whole-of-life policies, these are unit-linked. Instead of investing in an underlying insurance fund, premiums are paid into one or more unit trusts. These are more exposed to stocks and shares than a typical insurance fund – as well as being much smaller – and this makes them slightly more volatile than with-profits contracts.

The value of the units your regular premiums buy can change almost daily. With a large insurance fund it takes much longer for market changes to filter through. The advantage unit-linking offers whole-of-life contracts is in the flexibility it allows. With these plans the policyholder can choose to split the regular premium between life cover and savings. The ratio of life cover to savings can be varied – although sometimes only at certain points during the policy term – in accordance with your changing needs. In theory you need only one policy to last your entire life. At the start of your working life, with only a small amount of income and no major financial responsibilities you could buy a universal policy giving you basic life cover. Later, as you become more affluent and your insurance needs grow, the policy can expand to cope with your changing circumstances. The level of insurance cover could be increased – often without the need for further medical evidence.

The value of your savings with any unit-linked contract depends on the value of the underlying stocks and shares at any given time. This is fine when the stock market is doing well, but not so good if it is falling. During the 1980s unit trusts did extremely well, and many apparently well-informed observers wondered why anyone would choose anything other than an equity-based investment. The answer became clear following the stock market crash of October 1987, and even more so from 1990 to 1992 when the recession caused funds to underperform. Some caution is therefore necessary when considering this type of policy for savings and insurance.

This caution may be reflected in the relatively low number of people buying flexible life plans. When it first arrived in the UK, universal life assurance was heralded as the all-singing, all-dancing policy. It was first marketed in the USA following the development of computer software making it simpler to administer flexible policies. Some believed that within a few years it would be the only type of life assurance anyone would buy. But that never happened. During the last few years numerous reasons have been put forward for the failure of flexible life to take off: anything from poor marketing by insurance companies to low commission payments for financial advisers.

My own view is that flexible policies are not all they are cracked up to be. Although they tend to be dressed up in all sorts of consumer benefits, these seem to be more beneficial to the insurer than the policyholder. All insurance companies want to take care of all your insurance needs. One of the best ways to do this is to lock you into a policy which appears to be whatever you want it to be. And what a universal life contract really is is a package of different insurance products from the same company.

If you compare the various elements of a particular flexible life package with separate policies offered by other companies, you may well find it makes more sense to chop and change policies and companies as the need arises. For example, if you take out a flexible whole-of-life policy at the age of twenty, you may choose the policy offering the highest level of life assurance at the lowest premium. But the same company's premiums may not be so competitive as you get older. So when your policy comes up for renewal after five years, or when you convert it to another type of policy, you could end up paying more than if you went to another company.

The same applies to the various types of policy insurance companies offer. Just because a company heads the market with term assurance rates, it doesn't necessarily follow that it will be the best for whole-of-life cover or endowments. Having said that, gay men may be attracted to by the ability to alter the policy without providing further evidence of health. This can be extremely useful but, not surprisingly, it has certain limits. There is often a restriction on when you can alter your policy: sometimes, for example, such changes have to coincide with particular events like buying a house. There will also probably be a limit to the amount of extra insurance cover you can get without having to provide evidence of your continuing good health.

Term assurance

Term assurance is the next step up the insurance ladder, and is probably the most common type of life assurance. It has the same with-profits and without-profits alternatives as does whole-of-life, but with much more besides.

Instead of providing life cover for the rest of the policy-holder's life, term assurance covers a specific period. This has two advantages. First, it is cheaper than whole-of-life because the insurance company is taking a smaller risk. If, for example, you buy a 20-year life policy there is a good chance that the insurance company will never have to pay out. Second, it means you can take out cover when you need it most. In everyone's life there are times when their financial responsibilities are greater than in others. Those with mortgages or who have dependants will want to make sure their commitments are met after they die. But the level of such commitment is unlikely to remain at the same level throughout your life. At some point, for example, your mortgage will be paid off. Because of its range of possible applications, there are various types of term assurance designed to meet certain needs.

Decreasing term assurance

Decreasing term assurance is usually used to insure loans – especially mortgages. Even if you feel you have no need for life assurance, lenders frequently make loans conditional on your buying it. Sometimes, as with a mortgage, they will insist that you assign the policy to them. This means that the lender will hold on to the actual policy document and all you receive is a copy. If you die during the policy term, the proceeds from the policy will automatically be used to repay the loan. Anything left over will be paid to your estate.

Decreasing term assurance differs from other types of term assurance because the level of cover it provides gradually reduces. This makes it best suited to loans where the regular repayments consist of interest plus a portion of the loan itself. With these, the amount you owe steadily reduces from the first repayment to the last. So the level of insurance cover required clearly reduces as well. Although there is nothing to stop you buying a term assurance contract to do the job, it would be more expensive than a decreasing term policy and would add to the overall cost of the loan.

Family income assurance

Family income assurance is another type of term assurance contract. In spite of its name, it can be useful whether or not you have a family. It is broadly the same as any other term assurance except that instead of paying out a cash lump sum it provides your dependants with a regular tax-free income after you die. With some policies, income payments will continue for a specified period no matter when you die during the term of the policy. There is a cheaper version, effectively based on a decreasing term assurance, with which if you die during the term of the policy, income will still be paid but only until the date the policy was due to finish. This, again, can be a useful cost-cutting measure if you have specific liabilities you want the loan to cover. Most family income policies also give the beneficiaries the right to convert the income to a lump sum if they prefer.

Convertible and renewable assurance

As with whole-of-life products, term assurance can also be fairly flexible. For some people it may not be so easy to predict how their future insurance needs may change. Rather than be locked into a policy with a specific term and cover they may prefer a more flexible approach.

Convertible and renewable policies can provide this. Convertible term assurance allows the policyholder to switch to another type of policy with the same company at any time during the term – usually without requiring any further evidence of your health or lifestyle. There are, though, several restrictions on how this option can be used. First, you may be limited to the range of the company's other products you can have access to. Make sure that you have a clear idea of what's on offer before committing yourself. Second, most companies place a limit on the age at which you can convert the policy. This is usually around retirement age – between sixty and sixty-five. Third, if you use the convertible option, the premium of your new policy will be based on your age at the time of conversion.

Renewable term assurance policies are usually convertible too, but also include an option to renew the policy at the end of the term without further evidence of health. The renewal periods tend to be quite short – about five years – and such policies often carry the same age restrictions as convertible plans.

Some add-on benefits

For a while during the 1980s there was a trend towards selling life assurance with what was called a guaranteed insurability option. This gave policyholders the right to increase their life cover without having to provide further medical evidence. Like several other 'add-on' benefits, it became increasingly available on policies other than the flexible varieties mentioned above. There are still some companies prepared to offer it, but because of the Aids risk the trend is no longer upwards.

As with flexible life plans, the option to extend can usually be exercised at certain points during the policy's term: at five- or ten-year intervals, or on occasions such as buying a house, getting married, or having a first child. Given the general attitude of insurance companies towards gay men and lesbians, it is extremely unlikely that they will recognize gay marriages or adoption by gay couples as 'special' occasions.

The amount by which life cover can be increased without further medical evidence is generally limited to a percentage of the initial amount. There is also usually a ceiling on the total amount of extra cover you can have, perhaps 50 or 100 per cent of the initial sum assured.

Another typical add-on benefit with many life policies is waiver of premium. Very often, for either health or financial reasons, people find it difficult to continue paying the premiums on a life policy. Waiver of premium can take two forms. Either the insurer will allow the insured to stop paying premiums for a limited period without reducing the level of cover or, under some circumstances, it will waive the premiums altogether. Without the waiver there are two main risks. Either the policy could be cancelled, or the benefits could be reduced to match the total level of premiums you have paid into the plan. Unfortunately, waiver of premium does not cover HIV.

Keyman

Gay men in business may have different life assurance needs from individuals. Often, when the nature of the business makes two individuals financially dependent on each other, some type of cover is needed to ensure that if one business partner dies the other will not lose money. It is only under these circumstances that individuals who are not related to each other can cross-propose life policies. This means that instead of having a policy where the owner and the beneficiary are the same person, one person can own a policy insuring another person's life.

One type of insurance that is increasingly popular is keyman insurance. This is usually appropriate to a commercial situation where the loss of a partner or employee would cause tangible financial problems for a business. A key individual would typically be someone with particular expertise who could not be replaced simply by employing someone else. Such policies can be bought on their own or, very often, included as part of another life policy.

Life assurance as savings

We have already touched briefly on the possibility of using assurance policies as savings plans in discussing universal plans. In fact, there are various other plans giving you life cover and some money back at the end of the term. One of the biggest weaknesses of most insurance policies is that it can seem expensive if you never have to make a claim. With life assurance you can feel even more hard done by because all the hard-earned premiums you paid in inevitably provide for someone else after you die. By introducing a savings element to your life assurance you can mitigate the premium cost and secure yourself some useful tax-free cash at a later date.

Endowment policies

The most common form of savings policy is the endowment, usually used to back interest-only mortgages. As with many insurance contracts, the premium you pay is pooled with other policyholders' money in the insurance company's life fund. It is then invested on your behalf by the fund manager into relatively safe gilts and bonds, although some funds have moved towards more volatile equities.

As a with-profits fund grows, bonuses are added to the initial sum assured on your policy in the same way as for with-profits, whole-of-life, and term assurance policies. The difference here is that, instead of paying out when you die, the policy pays out on maturity. If the money is invested for more than 10 years this payout will be free of any income tax or capital gains tax and will not affect any other tax allowances you have.

Understandably, the premiums for this type of policy are a lot higher than for straightforward life cover. Their efficiency has also been called into question during recent years. During the boom years of the 1980s, endowment plans were extremely popular mainly because they were safe investments providing a better return than the bank or building society. The only drawback was the lack of access to your money. Few people worried about this until bonus rates started to fall at the beginning of the 1990s.

There are several facts about endowments that need to be considered before investing in one. For the remainder of the 1990s it is unlikely that insurance funds will again find the level of returns they enjoyed in the 1980s. Therefore past performance figures for a lot of insurance companies could be an unreliable indicator of how the endowment will do in future.

Next is the matter of insurance company charges. Since the Financial Services Act became law, various interests have attempted to force insurance companies to be more open about the profit they make on endowment policies. To date, the powerful insurance industry lobby has ensured that their hefty charges remain a secret. So although independent advisers are obliged to let you know how much of your premium is paid to them in commission, insurance companies – and more especially their direct salesmen – do not.

But the extent of their charges becomes clear when you look at how much of your money is returned if you cancel the endowment before the maturity date. Even the most reputable companies will probably pay back nothing if the policy is less than two years old. With some companies, policies have to be older still before they offer a cash surrender value. This means that all the premiums you pay during the early years of an endowment are completely swallowed up in charges.

When policies do eventually show a value you will still be heavily penalized if you attempt to cash them in before the end of the term. Figures for the number of policies surrendered before maturity can only be guessed at, but some sources put the figure at 70 per cent. Unless bonus rates start to recover, few people will regard the disadvantages of savings endowments as being outweighed by the advantages.

Maximum investment plans

Maximum investment plans offer an alternative. MIPs only just satisfy the Inland Revenue's criteria for what a life policy must be in order for its proceeds to be free of any tax liability. These criteria are that the policy must be written for a period of no less than ten years, with premiums payable at least annually, and that the sum assured should equal at least 75 per cent of the total premiums payable over the term. So, if you were to pay £100 a month into a MIP with a ten-year term, the sum assured would have to be £9000. This small amount of life cover will account for a minimal proportion of the total premium. The rest will be invested in a range of underlying unit trusts.

Unit trusts, because they are mainly equity-based, are more volatile than the insurance funds in which the premiums of more typical endowment policies are invested. Although this increases the investment risk, it also increases the chances of making much larger gains. In any case, statistics generally show that those invested over a long term in equities have historically fared better than those with other types of savings. Provided you are not hoping to make a lot of money very quickly, equities usually prove to be a steady bet.

MIP investors have the added advantage of being able to switch between the underlying unit trusts. With most MIPs, the different unit trusts in which they are invested represent varying degrees of risk and reward. You can happily switch between the various unit trusts in accordance with how confident you feel about the market. While the first few switches may be free of charge, however, most managers will expect you to pay after having made a certain number. If you plan on actively managing your MIP, such charges can become fairly expensive and can quickly outpace any gains such switches might make you.

More important than the range of funds you can invest in is their quality. Some managers are not incapable of using things like MIPs as a way of drawing investors into otherwise unpopular unit trusts, so check the performance of the unit trusts on offer in the 'Managed Funds' section of the *Financial Times*. The other important thing to consider is the cost. Unlike typical endowment policies, unit-linked plans have a transparent charging structure. This does not necessarily mean they will be more reasonable. Check with your adviser about all the possible charges.

Another advantage that MIPs or any other type of unit-linked investment have over endowments is their cash surrender value. The value of the units you buy will depend entirely on the state of the value of the trust on the day you sell it. Should you need to gain access to your savings, for whatever reason, before the term of the policy expires, you can do so without incurring huge penalties. There are only really two provisos. One is that, if possible, you should try to cash in your units when the underlying unit trusts are performing well. The other is that early encashment could make you liable to either income tax or capital gains tax.

Buying a policy

Having decided what type of insurance policy you need, the first obstacle to actually getting it is the application form – known by insurers as the proposal. These used to be quite straightforward. The insurance company simply needs to know about your age, sex, and general health; from this it works out how much your policy should cost.

Previously, if there was anything out of the ordinary on the proposal, the insurer might ask for more information. If you were five feet tall and weighed twenty stone, or if you had a pre-existing illness, the insurance company would either ask your doctor for more details or send you to one of the doctors on its panel for a medical. All this still applies, but insurance companies now consider being gay a health risk too. So even answers on the proposal form which only mildly hint at your sexuality will send the insurance company into a panic.

Most single men risk being weeded out for closer inspection – particularly if they live with another single man. So too is anyone previously infected with a sexually transmitted disease or anyone who has visited a part of the world with a high level of HIV infection, like Africa or Southeast

Asia. If you have ever taken an HIV test, you are sure to attract extra attention. Even if the test was negative, the company will consider it an indicator of a high-risk lifestyle rather than a sign of how safe you are. If you are HIV positive, your proposal will be turned down outright.

Depending on the individual insurance company, there are a number of ways they might react to any of these answers. In most cases you will be sent a lifestyle questionnaire. These nasty intrusive forms ask more direct questions about your sexual activity and general lifestyle. Depending on your answers and the attitude of the insurance company you have chosen, there are a number of possible outcomes. You may be refused life cover altogether. This could also result in your name being added to the Impaired Lives Register, which could prevent you from applying for insurance from another company (p. 169). Even if you manage to avoid this list, with any life assurance applications you make elsewhere you will inevitably be asked if you have ever been refused insurance.

When insurance companies first woke up to HIV in the late 1980s, simply being gay meant you would definitely be refused life assurance. This attitude was widely condemned, and insurance companies are now claiming to be more relaxed about gay men. In some cases this is simply a public relations exercise. Only a couple of years ago the chief underwriter with the Clerical Medical insurance company, Peter Gibbs, was quoted in the finance magazine *Money Week* as saying, 'I would be delighted if a homosexual never came near us again for a policy. If homosexual clients of ours cancel existing policies, even better.' So much for the new climate of enlightenment.

But some progress has been made, even though things are still far from ideal. This has more to do with the economic problems some companies have suffered during recent years rather than any genuine relaxation of their anti-gay stance. Thanks to nose-diving profits and an increasingly competitive insurance market, companies are coming to appreciate the wastefulness of ignoring a sizeable and affluent social minority. It may be interesting to see whether or not companies become more discriminating again now that profitability is returning to the insurance market.

The upshot is that there are companies now that will insure gay men. That's the good news. The bad news is that you will probably be expected to stump up a higher than usual premium. This 'loading' can be up to 250 per cent more than the premium paid by a heterosexual man of similar age and fitness. What makes this all the more galling is that towards the end of the 1980s insurance companies used HIV scaremongering as an excuse to increase male life assurance premiums by 125 per cent. This, they said, was to cover themselves against an Aids liability they had already unwittingly taken on. But as they undoubtedly overestimated the damage Aids would cause them during the last few years, and that you will get life assurance only if the company believes you are probably less of a health risk than most heterosexuals, any kind of loading is an outrage.

There are really only two ways of avoiding these problems completely. One is not to bother with life assurance at all; the other is to lie about your sexuality. Neither is a practical solution. Even those who feel no particular urge to buy life assurance will, at some stage, find themselves in a situation where they need to have it. As we have seen in previous chapters, pensions, loans, mortgages, healthcare, savings, and various other types of financial instrument can all include at least an element of life cover.

Lying on a proposal form is a really bad idea. Lots of gay men have done it simply to obtain mortgages and pensions. In fact it can prove to be an absolute minefield. As we have seen, insurance companies need to know all the ins and outs before they deign to take your money. If you can pass this stage without being given away by your doctor, you can be certain the insurance company will be even more scrupulous before paying out. If you die, even from something totally unrelated to Aids, and the insurance company finds that you were less than honest on the proposal form, it will probably refuse to pay out. In the meantime it will probably hang on to all the money you paid in.

The most practical solution is to tackle the insurance problem head-on. Start by finding a trustworthy independent financial adviser to do the job for you. A good adviser who is used to handling insurance for gay men will know which companies are most likely to insure gay men and which ones should be avoided.

Independent advisers, as opposed to tied agents, are legally obliged to register with FIMBRA (the Financial Intermediaries, Managers, and Brokers Regulatory Authority). Call them on 071-538 8860, and ask them to send you a list of registered advisers in your area. Unfortunately, FIMBRA is unlikely to have much of an idea about which advisers specialize in gay finance. There are, however, several FIMBRA registered advisers who advertise in the gay press. If possible, ask around to see if anyone you know has a trustworthy adviser they can recommend.

The Single European Market

The Single European Market officially came into being on 1 January 1993. Its aim is to allow the free movement of goods, services, and finance throughout the European Community. Unfortunately this does not yet apply to insurance. Regulations governing the sale of policies across EC borders are due to be put in place by July 1994. After then, insurance companies will be able to ply their trade anywhere in the EC.

The question for gay men is whether or not more liberal trade will make access to life cover any easier. The brutal answer is that it probably will not. There is some hope that competition from foreign companies in the UK market will cause insurance companies to behave less prejudicially towards gay men. Unfortunately there is as yet no indication that insurance companies from other EC countries will compete in the UK market at all. In spite of recent hikes in premium costs in the UK, life assurance here is largely considered to be cheaper than in other parts of Europe. Whether or not this will change remains to be seen. People in the UK, of course, are already free to buy life assurance anywhere in the EC. But even if you can overcome the problems of distance and language to find a competitively priced policy, European companies are unlikely to be any more keen on insuring gay men than UK insurers are.

A policy for your needs

The type of life cover you choose will depend mainly on your personal circumstances and on what areas of your finances you wish to protect. If you have dependants – a non-working partner, or children – the need to make a lump sum or regular income available if you die is clearly greater than if you have only yourself to look after. The need for insurance increases whenever you acquire a new financial responsibility like a mortgage or some other type of loan.

Ideally you should opt for the policy providing the cover you want as cheaply as possible. There's no point in buying a whole-of-life policy, for example, if you want life cover for a loan that will be paid back in ten years – unless you have other reasons for wanting to be insured for the rest of your life. Whatever your needs, one of the policies mentioned in this chapter will fit the bill.

However, if you are HIV positive you will find many financial doors closed to you. But there are ways around the problem, as we shall see in the last chapter.

8
POSITIVE

The financial problems facing gay people who are diagnosed HIV positive are clearly very different from those of others who fall ill. As soon as the diagnosis is made, a wide number of financial options disappear. This is especially true of the various types of health and life assurance. In fact it is the enduring irony of insurance that people who need insurance most are denied it.

One of the greatest needs of those who are HIV positive is to raise cash. This may not be apparent at first, but it may become so as time goes on. Certainly a large number of people with HIV are able to continue working for almost the entire duration of the infection, either because the virus has little or no physical effect or because the nature of the person's work allows them to cover up periods of absence.

In many cases the trauma of the diagnosis itself is enough to make the very idea of working anathema. In my view this is as valid a reason for stopping work as any debilitating physical impairments. Whether or not the Department of Social Security will agree is another matter, but a sympathetic letter from a doctor is often enough to get the ball rolling as far as state benefits are concerned.

Much depends on each individual's way of dealing with the illness. Some may cope by throwing themselves wholeheartedly into their jobs, others may prefer to take time out to come to terms with the way their lives have changed. But no matter how the disease is dealt with, one certainty is that bills will keep arriving even though your income may have dried up. In some cases even more money may be needed to cover the cost of, say, adapting the home or moving house. Some employers may be willing to cover all or part of a sick employee's salary for a while, but this will not continue for good.

Health insurance

All medical insurance and permanent health insurance taken out during the last few years will exclude treatment for HIV related illnesses. Even medical complaints that are obviously nothing to do with the disease are bound to be caught up in this general exclusion. The only exception may be policies that were taken out earlier than 1987 when insurance companies were less panicky about HIV. In any case, if you have a PHI policy that is a few years old, take it along to your financial adviser and have the fine print checked out. If you find there is no specific HIV exclusion, make sure there is also nothing there that allows the insurer to change the terms of the policy without prior warning. Several companies include such a clause, and use it as a let-out from HIV related claims.

Although an insurance company may reserve the right to change some terms and conditions of a policy, the 'permanent' in the PHI name means that once the policy has been started it cannot be cancelled – regardless of how the policyholder's health or lifestyle changes. The only exception may be where the policyholder takes up a new occupation which is more dangerous than the last. Beware, though, because some companies have started selling short-term and reviewable PHI policies in order to get round the 'permanent' obligation.

The heavy claims experience of some health insurers has caused them to clamp down on claims. One or two have even employed 'medical' staff whose job is to monitor the condition of those who are already receiving payments from them. If the company doctor believes you are able to work in spite of your illness – regardless of the opinion of an independent doctor – then your claim may be disallowed. Your independent financial adviser will be able to identify the companies with a history of treating claimants in this way.

LIFE ASSURANCE

If you already have a life assurance policy that is at least a few years old, there is a chance that it will have an accrued value. Even a pure life assurance policy, one which normally has a value only when the insured person dies, can sometimes be turned into cash.

Cash surrender

An endowment policy, the type of policy which has an investment element, can simply be cashed in with the insurance company you bought it from. The amount you get back will depend on a number of factors such as the length of time you have owned the policy and how much bonus has been added. In some cases, especially with policies that are only a few years old, there may be no cash surrender value at all. This is because during the early years of a policy most of your contributions are used to pay the life company's charges.

When the policy does have a cash surrender value that value could be less than the total amount you have paid in, even if the time is fairly close to the policy's maturity date. This is because insurance companies frequently apply penalties to policies that are cashed in early. Also, from a tax viewpoint, policies have to be in force for at least ten years for the proceeds to be paid free of tax. If you surrender the policy in less than ten years, you may be landed with a tax bill.

In spite of the possible drawbacks, there is no harm in asking the insurance company to tell you how much your policy is worth. Some insurance companies offer a better deal than others and you may be pleasantly surprised. But if surrendering an endowment policy appears to be a poor option, there are alternatives.

Auctioning your policy

Many types of insurance policy have an inherent value. For endowment policies this is the maturity value plus the death benefit; for whole-of-life policies it is the death benefit only.

A growing number of investors are coming to see that buying a second-hand policy can be extremely profitable. They agree to pay the policyholder a cash sum, and take over any remaining premium payments. In return they will receive the tax-free cash payout at the end of the policy's term. Auctions of such policies are held regularly, and usually secure more cash for the policyholder than a cash surrender would. Your financial adviser will be able to put you in touch with several reputable auction houses.

Selling the death value

This is a variation on the above theme, and is a way of raising cash on a pure life policy which otherwise would have no value until the day you die. Instead of buying the investment value on the policy, the investor buys the life cover. The policyholder is paid a cash sum by the investor who, in turn, makes a claim against the insurance company when the policyholder dies.

The idea of a complete stranger having a financial interest in your death sounds like a plot for a thriller, and may seem a bit spooky. In fact it can be an excellent way of raising money just when you need it most – even if you are likely to be telephoned regularly to see whether or not you are still alive. The buyer takes over any regular premium payments and you are paid between 50 per cent and 80 per cent of the sum assured.

In the UK, this service is offered by a company set up in 1992 called Life Benefit Resources, which buys most types of life policy from anyone diagnosed as having a life expectancy of two years or less. At the time of writing, the company was looking at the viability of pushing this limit up to three years. It claims to have paid out an average 69.4 per cent of the insurance value of policies it has bought so far.

Accelerated life cover

For those who are diagnosed as terminally ill, more and more companies are prepared to pay out life assurance claims *before* the policyholder dies. When you think about it, this makes sound business sense from the insurer's viewpoint. The idea of life assurance paying out before you die is an attractive add-on benefit for those looking for cover, and it adds nothing to the cost of the policy.

This growing trend can be especially beneficial for those diagnosed as HIV positive. If the virus develops into Aids, such policies provide the full amount of life cover exactly when it is most needed. The other ways of raising cash from existing policies described so far invariably pay out only a percentage of the full insurance value.

PERSONAL PENSION PLANS

If you have a personal pension, it may be possible to take the benefits before the usual retirement age if you become too ill to work. Provided the scheme's trustees receive written confirmation from a doctor that the pension plan owner is unable to work, they can agree to pay out 25 per cent of the accrued fund as a tax-free lump sum and use the balance to provide a regular pension immediately.

Unfortunately, and in spite of the pension plan owner's poor health, the insurance company with which the plan is arranged will inevitably assume that the person receiving the pension will live well into old age. So if the total fund is only £10,000, say, this will provide a £2500 lump sum, while the remaining £7500 will probably translate into a regular pension of a few hundred pounds a year. The insurance company is, sadly, unlikely to be compassionate enough to take individual circumstances into consideration.

Anyone finding themselves in this situation should consult an independent financial adviser to find out how to use their free-market option. By law, anyone in a pension scheme can take their accrued fund to any of the many pension providers in the UK market to see which one offers the best deal. A financial adviser will be able to tell you which companies are paying the best pensions.

Waiver of premium

Many pension plans (and life assurance policies) offer waiver-of-premium benefit for those who are too ill to continue working. While this does not provide any cash, your pension or assurance policy will continue accruing benefits – at least for a while. Unfortunately, newer plans have an HIV exclusion clause. As with all modern income protection plans, this exclusion means that even if you are disabled after being hit by a bus, you will be prevented from making a claim if you are HIV positive.

Company pensions

People in occupational pension schemes may also be able to take their pension benefits earlier. Under occupational pension rules the trustees can pay out your entire portion of the pension fund if you have a reduced life expectancy (usually of three years or less). Unfortunately, this requires you to explain your illness to your employer – something many HIV sufferers may not feel comfortable about.

Remortgaging property

If you own your home outright, or if it is worth significantly more than you owe on it, it is easy to arrange a remortgage giving you extra cash provided you are still working. Life assurance is not always demanded by mortgage lenders, so someone with HIV can usually organize a loan as easily as anyone else. Make sure, too, that the remortgage is interest-only rather than a repayment loan. With a repayment mortgage, a portion of each monthly repayment is considered to be part of the loan itself, and would not be covered by state benefits if the borrower became too ill to work.

Unfortunately there is a Catch 22 for those raising cash in this way. If the borrower is too ill to work, the DSS will normally cover the interest payments on a home loan (50 per cent for the first 16 weeks and then 100 per cent up to a maximum of £150,000). But anyone with more than £8000 in savings is disqualified from receiving this benefit. You could end up using the money you borrowed to pay for the money you borrowed.

There are, of course, ways of making the money 'disappear'. It could be 'gifted' to a friend under PET rules (see Chapter 2), with the added benefit of reducing the likelihood of your estate being hit by inheritance tax after you die. Be careful, though, to ensure that whatever you do is legal. Simply depositing the cash in an undeclared offshore bank account would be considered fraudulent, and no reputable financial adviser would recommend it.

Dying in debt

Some people have the idea that, for people with HIV, or any other potentially fatal illness, getting into debt is a way of raising cash which will never have to be paid back. The widespread use of hire purchase, credit cards, store cards, and bank loans gives people the opportunity to pile up huge debts. Several facts should be considered, though, before racing off to Selfridges with your platinum card:

• With the accelerating pace of medical advances there is a chance of surviving the virus longer than expected. On top of the continuing illness, a growing debt burden will only aggravate an already stressful situation.

• The debt will remain after you die. Partners, though not usually legally compelled to repay such loans, often feel morally obliged to do so. I have known surviving partners to be financially hamstrung for years by such debts.

• In addition, everything you own when you die will be sold to repay creditors before any assets are distributed in the way described in your will (see Chapter 1). Dependants you intended providing for after your death could suffer as a result.

All in all, this is the least desirable way of raising money and should be avoided. Naturally, though, there will be people who consider it appropriate, and perhaps the only possible way of raising much needed money.

However, even if you are diagnosed HIV positive, there is no need to rush straight to a financial adviser and begin looking at ways of raising cash. If the necessity to raise cash does arise, it will usually be later rather than sooner.

APPENDIX:
FINANCIAL ADVICE

Although this guide has outlined the problems of gay finance and offered solutions, it should ideally be viewed as an adjunct to advice from an independent financial adviser. While the guide can deal with some of the broader issues and give you an idea of how your finances should be arranged, a professional adviser will help you with the details, and will also be able to keep you updated on any recent changes – especially if previously reluctant insurers and finance companies relax their attitudes to gay men.

There are those who would argue that impartial advice from so-called professionals carries its own risks. At the time of writing, the Securities and Investments Board had just launched an investigation into the way private pensions have been sold in the UK since they were introduced in 1988. In spite of the protection supposedly offered by the 1986 Financial Services Act, up to 400,000 people may have been wrongly encouraged to leave their company pension schemes and contribute to a personal pension plan instead.

With this latest horror story, and previous tales of investors defrauded by the likes of finance firms Barlow Clowes and the Levitt Group, it is little wonder that many people would rather talk to relatives and friends about their finances than turn to a professional. Aunt Mabel may not know much about finance, but at least she wouldn't recommend putting your life savings into US junk bonds. But the UK personal finance industry is heavily regulated. By following a few basic steps you should be able to find a good and reliable adviser.

Choosing an adviser

Finding a financial adviser who is used to dealing with gay finance is one of the hurdles gay men face. The vast majority will have far less idea than you do of the particular needs of gay men. The obvious place to look is in the gay press, where financial advisers frequently advertise their services. Unfortunately this is no guarantee of their ability. The financial services industry has become especially cut-throat in recent years, heavy regulation and a slump in business forcing advisers into a broader search for new business. Several have been attracted by the supposedly high level of disposable income within the gay community, and have set themselves up as gay finance specialists. In fact they usually have absolutely no idea of the real problems gay men face.

Luckily, few of the advisers who target themselves at gay people purely to increase their turnover last for very long. Very soon they realize they have overstepped the mark and return whence they came. So one useful way of checking an adviser's credentials is to see how long they have been handling gay business. Better still, take a recommendation from someone who has already found a skilful and reliable financial adviser.

Tied advisers

Personal finance has become heavily regulated in the last few years. There are now numerous ways for people to ensure that the advice they receive is good, or to do something about it if it is not. Since 1988, financial advisers have had to identify themselves as one of two types: tied or independent. Tied advisers come in various shapes and sizes. They may call themselves tied agents, tied representatives, company representatives, or what have you, but what they all have in common is their association with a particular finance company – usually an insurance company, a bank, or a building society.

Either tied advisers are employees of such companies, or they have an exclusive arrangement whereby they sell only that company's products. While the advice they offer you may be wide and varied, the products they sell are not: they can sell you only the products of one company. These products may be some of the best on the market, offering impressive investment returns, low management charges, and competitive premiums. Unfortunately the only word you have for that is the tied agent's. If you ask him about personal pension plans, he is unlikely to tell you that Whizzo Finance in the high street offers a superior one to his.

Independent advisers

For these reasons, the quality of tied financial advice has been heavily scrutinized lately. Most people agree that independent advice, in principle at least, is the best. Independent advisers are those with no company affiliations. If you tell them you want the best performing pension in the market, they can usually sell it to you. They are also obliged to let you know how much their advice will cost you.

Very often advisers like to give the impression their advice is free. And in a way it is: you can usually go and

chat with an adviser for hours without it costing you a
penny. But when you decide to buy something, a portion of
the cost will go to the adviser as commission. Independent
advisers have to let you know how much this is. If an
adviser were to sell you something other than the product
best suited to your financial needs because a worse company paid a better commission, he would be breaking the
law. So far, tied agents have been under no pressure to
tell you how much their advice costs. The powerful UK
insurance lobby claims that it would be impossible to
work out what percentage of the cost of each policy is
swallowed up in expenses. So far, the regulators have
believed them.

Fees

A small proportion of advisers charge fees. These are
usually solicitors or accountants offering financial advice
alongside their usual services. They may be tied or independent. Paying for advice can sometimes be extremely cost
effective, even though the benefits may not be immediately
obvious. It may also guarantee the impartiality of your
adviser. Fee-charging advisers will usually waive their right
to any commission on whatever they sell you. Because they
know they will be paid for their advice and not what they
sell you, there is less chance of you being sold something
you do not need just because it pays the adviser
commission.

Unfortunately, not all fee-charging advisers are utterly
scrupulous. If you do pay a fee, make sure the adviser
intends refunding you the commission. You should also be
wary if it is suggested that you sign a client agreement

setting out the terms on which advice will be given. During the last couple of years, the courts have heard numerous cases in which clients have been charged huge amounts after receiving little or no advice. A nasty client agreement I once saw gave the adviser *carte blanche* to send insurance quotations to his client whenever he wanted. What the client failed to realize – until it was too late – was that each quotation he received incurred a fee. Before he knew it he was being sued for a large sum of money, even though he had taken up none of the quotations he was offered.

Be wary of an otherwise fee-charging adviser who offers to waive his fees in lieu of commission received for any products you buy. The tacit understanding here is that if you buy nothing, you pay nothing. Very often this can work quite well, but complications can set in if you agree to buy a particular product but change your mind shortly after. Your client agreement may make you liable for the commission the adviser would have received had you carried on with the plan. The financial regulators seem unclear about how to deal with this. Some believe such agreements are illegal. Under the Financial Services Act all of us have a 30-day cooling-off period following the purchase of any financial product. At any point during that time you can cancel the policy and have any premiums you have paid refunded. Some companies offer a more generous cooling-off period. If your adviser insists that you pay commission for a policy you have cancelled then, it may be argued, you are being unfairly discouraged from cancelling it. Others would point out that the payment owed is for advice and not for the product itself. While this issue remains unresolved, it is safest to check the wording of any agreement you are asked to sign. If you have any doubts at all, do not sign – make your excuses and go elsewhere.

Best advice

Advisers must make it immediately clear whether their advice is tied or independent. To do this they should present you with a 'buyer's guide'. This is a standard brochure explaining the difference between the two types of advice.

Whichever type of adviser you choose has to operate within strict guidelines. At your first meeting he must carry out a 'fact-find'. This is called various things by different advisers, but whatever its name, its aim is to create an official record of your financial needs. You will be asked how much you earn, who is dependent on your income, what your financial outgoings are, what insurance and savings plans you already have, and so on. The adviser can then indicate areas where your financial plans are lacking. For example, your job may not provide you with any pension benefits even though you are only 15 years from retirement. He can then recommend a suitable plan, and can ensure that it fits in comfortably with your budget.

Whatever recommendations the adviser makes must conform to the principles of 'best advice'. This means you should be offered only those products suited to your financial needs, and not products paying the adviser the most money. Each fact-find must be kept on file at the adviser's office. If you complain later that you were ripped off, it will be consulted.

It is also strictly against the law for an adviser to recommend that you cancel any existing arrangements you have if this is not 'best advice'. He cannot, for example, look at your completed fact-find and conclude that you should replace an insurance policy you have had for some time with one he can sell you. This was a common ruse with many door-to-door insurance salesmen before they were regulated.

Having made a recommendation based on your initial meeting, advisers are not allowed to put you under pressure to take it. This ban covers more subtle persuasion as well as the traditional foot-in-the-door technique: advisers are not supposed to promise you a free carriage clock or a weekend in Scunthorpe as an incentive. And if you reject an adviser's idea completely, he cannot approach you later with the same idea again.

Cold calling

This is another area where the public now has more rights than before the Financial Services Act became law. A cold call is simply an uninvited approach from a financial adviser. A familiar scenario is opening the front door and finding a pair of insurance salesmen standing there. Your initial relief that they are not Jehovah's Witnesses is quickly replaced by the realization they are not dispensed with as easily. Their first aim – as is drummed in to them on their brief training course – is to get into your home. It is much easier to slam your front door on them than to prise them out of a chair.

Once they have crossed your threshold, it will soon become clear that the easiest way to get shot of them is to sign on the dotted line and hand over a cheque. Okay, you can cancel the cheque and the policy, but it is far better not to let things get this far. Unless you are interested in their advice you should politely decline their opening gambit and shut your door. The law prevents them from bothering you a second time. If they persist, you should point this out. If they ignore you, report them to one of the financial services ombudsmen (whose addresses and telephone numbers are at the end of this appendix). The same applies to cold calling over the telephone.

Some advisers specializing in cold calling operate from plush offices in the business districts of big towns and cities. They employ an army of salesmen who use the telephone directory to find business prospects. Once they make contact, they encourage you to arrange a meeting with a salesman in their office.

Of course, some cold-calling advisers may be extremely good at what they do. Unfortunately, though, many of them employ high-pressure sales tactics aimed purely at selling policies. Inevitably, too, cold callers are tied agents offering the products of only one company. Even if they are independent, they are extremely unlikely to be well versed in gay finance. Allowing them to ferret through your financial affairs could lead to all sorts of problems.

As a general rule, it is worth remembering that the best advisers do not have to approach you for business. If you do feel you have been subjected to high-pressure selling or talked into an inappropriate contract, there are several things you can do.

How to complain

The first step is to complain directly to the company whose products the adviser has sold you. Sadly, even the most reputable companies have one or two dodgy salesmen and are often keen to identify them. They will often act quickly to correct the situation.

If the company refuses to acknowledge your complaint or ignores you, the next step is to approach the appropriate regulatory body for the company you wish to complain about. There are several organizations. The Life Assurance and Unit Trust Regulatory Organisation (LAUTRO) is responsible for the behaviour of tied agents. The Financial Intermediaries Managers and Brokers Regulatory Association (FIMBRA) deals with independent advisers. The Investment Managers Regulatory Organisation (IMRO) monitors companies investing money on your behalf. There are various others, but these three are the ones you are most likely to come across. In some cases, especially with accountants and solicitors who offer financial advice, complaints may be dealt with by the bodies that ordinarily deal with the other aspects of their businesses.

Any of these organizations will be able to tell you whether or not you have grounds for complaint. If you do, they will explain how to set the wheels in motion. In some cases there are ombudsmen you can approach directly with your complaint. The insurance ombudsman, for example, will look at any grievance involving an insurance company regardless of whether the business was handled by a tied or an independent adviser.

This range of regulatory bodies may appear confusing, and indeed steps are being taken to rationalize the system. Most importantly, the Securities and Investments Board (which oversees the regulation of financial services) would like to see all the separate regulators brought together under one grouping, to be called the Personal Investment Authority (PIA). This will be responsible for regulating all advisers, whether tied or independent, all insurance companies, unit trust companies, and investment managers. But at the time of writing the PIA is having trouble getting off the ground, and there are concerns that the differences between what are often conflicting interests will tear the whole thing apart.

Unregulated finance

One area of personal finance which is conspicuously free from the terms of the Financial Services Act is borrowing. When the Act was framed the regulators had the simple intention of protecting those who invest money, not those who borrow it. This has had the disturbing side-effect of pushing some former investment wide boys into the lending business.

While lenders are constrained by some legislation, they are not tethered by anything as far-reaching as the Financial Services Act. Advisers, for example, are not obliged to offer you best advice on loans. If they lumber you with an uncompetitive, high-interest loan because it pays them a high commission, there is nothing you can do about it. So although you should be cautious when entering into any financial arrangement, you should be doubly careful about loans. Luckily the government is aware of this shortfall in personal finance legislation, so the situation could change.

Addresses

FIMBRA
Hertsmere House, Hertsmere Road
London E14 4AB

Tel: 071-538 8860

LAUTRO
Centre Point, 103 New Oxford Street
London WC1A 1QH

Tel: 071-379 0444

IMRO
Broadwalk House, 5 Appold Street
London EC2A 2AA

Tel: 071-628 6022

INSURANCE OMBUDSMAN BUREAU
City Gate One, 135 Park Street
London SE1 9EA

Tel: 071-928 4488

SOLICITORS COMPLAINTS BUREAU
Victoria Court, 8 Dormer Place
Leamington Spa, Warwickshire CV32 5AE

Tel: 0926 822007

**INSTITUTE OF CHARTERED ACCOUNTANTS
IN ENGLAND AND WALES**
Professional Conduct Department, ICAEW
Gloucester House, 399 Silbury Boulevard
Central Milton Keynes MK9 2HL

Tel: 0908 248048

ABBREVIATIONS

AVC – Aditional Voluntary Contributions
BES – Business Expansion Scheme
CGT – Capital Gains Tax
COMPS – Contracted-Out Money Purchase Scheme
EIS – Enterprise Investment Scheme
EPP – Executive Pension Plan
FIMBRA – Financial Intermediaries Managers and
   Brokers Regulatory Authority
FSA – Financial Services Act
FSAVC – Free Standing Additional Voluntary
   Contributions
FTSE – Financial Times Stock Exchange (index)
LAPR – Life Assurance Premium Relief
MIP – Maximum Investment Plan
NI – National Insurance
PAYE – Pay As You Earn
PEP – Personal Equity Plan
PET – Potentially Exempt Trust
PHI – Permanent Health Insurance
PPP – Personal Pension Plan
PRAS – Pension Relief at Source
RPI – Retail Prices Index
SERPS – State Earnings Related Pension Scheme
SIB – Securities and Investments Board
SIPP – Self-Invested Personal Pension
SSAS – Small Self-Administered Scheme
TESSA – Tax Exempt Special Savings Account
USM – Unlisted Securities Market

INDEX
AND GLOSSARY

*in order to maximise the
investment element* – 183–5
Maxwell, Robert, 128
medical expenses insurance,
148–53
money purchase scheme – *pension
where the level of income is
determined by the amount of cash
available to buy an annuity at
retirement* – 114
Mortgage Interest Relief at Source
(MIRAS), 47–8, 57
mortgages, 44–69, 76–7;
centralized lenders, 53–5;
decreasing term assurance, 177;
indemnity policies, 50–3; life
assurance, 44–5; loans v. interest
rates, 66–9; mortgage protection
policies, 13; non-status, 49–50;
raising, 46–9; redemption
penalties, 54–5; remortgaging
property, 197–8; self-employed,
49; types, 55–66

National Health Service (NHS),
144, 145, 148, 153
National Insurance (NI), 112, 113,
114
National Savings, 41, 97
negative equity, 40
net relevant earnings, 123
nil-allocation units, 90
no-claims discounts, 151
non-smoker discounts, 151
non-status mortgage – *mortgage
where the lender requires no
proof of income; usually
dependent on a higher than
average deposit* – 49–50
nursing insurance, 152–3

offshore banking, 106–7
offshore fund – *investment fund
based in any area not subject to
UK taxes* – 103–6
old-age pension, 112
ombudsmen, 206–7, 208
open market option, 118–19

PAYE, 26–7, 113

pension mortgage – *interest-only
mortgage, similar to an
endowment mortgage, but where
the loan is repaid with a portion
of the tax-free lump sum
available on retirement to those
in personal pension plans* – 60–3
Pension Relief at Source (PRAS) –
*system allowing those in personal
pension plans to make their
contributions net of tax* – 119
pension trust – *a trust ensuring
your pension fund is paid to your
partner if you die before you
retire* – 22–3
pensions, 96, 109–43: Additional
Voluntary Contributions,
128–32; alternatives, 131–2;
calculation of benefits, 124–6;
cash benefit, 118; company,
122–32, 197; Contracted Out
Money Purchase Schemes,
122–3; contributions, 119–20;
death-in-service, 36–7, 126;
defined benefit schemes, 123–4;
deposit administration, 114–15;
earnings cap, 120, 133, 136–7;
executive pension plans, 135,
138–9; Expression of Wishes,
111–12; Free-Standing AVCs,
129–32; High Net Worth,
132–9; HIV-positive people,
196–7; life cover, 121; lump
sum, 125–6, 132; Maxwell and
the Goode Committee, 128; open
market option, 118–19; personal,
113–21; 196–7; self-
administered, 133–8; Self-
Invested Personal Pensions,
133–5; Small Self-Administered
Schemes (SSASs), 133, 135–8;
State Earnings Related Pension
Scheme (SERPS), 112–13, 114,
122; state pensions, 109, 110,
112–13; switching, 117–19;
unit-linked plans, 116–17;
with-profits contracts, 115–16,
117

trust *contd.*
governed by a legal document, similar to a will, to establish how the trust's assets should be disposed of – 18–23: insurance, 21–2; pension, 22–3; tax planning, 21

umbrella fund – *investment fund offering a range of sub funds for investors to choose from* – 104–6

Unfair Contracts (Terms) Act – *law aimed at preventing unfair contracts* – 171

unit-linked pension – *a fund investing in unit trusts* – 116–17

unit trust – *fund that pools cash from hundreds of investors and uses it to invest in stocks and shares; investors buy units which rise or fall in value depending on how the stock market is performing* – 87–92, 98: cash funds, 81; flexible whole-of-life assurance, 174–6; maximum investment plans, 184–5; mortgages, 60; portfolio services, 92–4

universal life assurance, 174–6

Unlisted Securities Market (USM) – *stocks and shares of companies not listed on the stock exchange* – 98

Venture Capital Trusts – *Government-sponsored scheme offering tax breaks for investment in venture capital funds* – 102–3

waiver-of-premium – *benefit offered on some life policies and health insurance whereby premiums will continue to be credited even if the policyholder becomes too ill to work and can no longer afford to pay them* – 111, 161, 180, 197

whole-of-life assurance – *life policy remaining in force for all of the policyholder's life* – 35–6, 172–6

wills, 6–18: children, 12, 15–17; DIY will-making, 8–11; living wills, 17–18; property, 11–13; residue, 13–14; solicitors, 14–15; witnesses, 8, 13–14

with-profits schemes – *life assurance or endowment policies benefiting from the addition of bonuses* – 115–16, 117, 172–3

witnesses, wills, 8, 13–14